BUILDING THE HAPPINESS-CENTRED BUSINESS

Business, Happiness and Money
Never Mixed ... Until Now

By Dr Paddi Lund

First published in 1994 by **Solutions Press**

149 Old Cleveland Road, Capalaba QLD 4157, Australia.
Telephone: (+61–7) 3823 3230
Facsimile: (+61–7) 3390 3610
E-mail: info@solutionspress.com.au
www.solutionspress.com.au

2nd edition published in 1997

Building the Happiness-Centred Business
ISBN 0 646 212 74 5

Designed and typeset by Australian Academic Press, Brisbane.
Printed by Shannon Books, Victoria

CONTENTS

APPRECIATION

Thank you to: my Mother for her editing, my father for his vegetables, Debra my love for her support and proof reading, Paul Dunn for unfailingly believing in my crazy ideas, Darryl Sturgess for his good advice and suggestions, Omer Reid for his vision, Stephen, Elke and Rose at AAP for their great typesetting and style improvements, and thanks most of all to Merilyn, Pat, Michelle, Kate, Sarah, Joanne and Elizabeth — my business family at PGL Dental Happiness. Their hard work and fortitude built the Happiness Centred Business.

PREAMBLE

Before you read *Building the Happiness-Centred Business* I would like to give you this gentle word of caution: this book is not quite as it may seem. At first glance Paddi may not appear to be a serious business writer, for Paddi's book looks a little like a novel, but do not be beguiled by his light, self-effacing style or the whimsical illustrations.

You are holding what some consider to be an important book.

It is not weighty or verbose. It is not pretentious or full of business wordiness. But it does contain a deep core of wisdom and truth that has helped many people steer an exciting new course for their business ... and their lives.

In the next few pages, listen to what prominent business authorities have to say, take their advice, and read this book carefully. While you will enjoy Paddi's quaint anecdotes, pay attention or you may miss out on some very valuable ideas.

Business Experts Agree

Unfortunately Paddi does not like to leave his comfortable happy business, so it is hard to persuade him to travel and present his ideas in public. We feel Paddi's story is so important that it should, as Mike Basch said, be 'trumpeted to the world'.

We would therefore like to express our gratitude to an increasing band of business consultants and speakers who have commended Paddi's work to their clients and told and retold Paddi's story.

Building the Happiness-Centred Buisness is meant for people in business, so who better to introduce Paddi's words than those who themselves teach business principles.

The consultants, writers and business trainers in the following pages are not just paying lip service. Most have at least recommended Paddi's book to friends and many have distributed his books to their own clients. Please let me introduce you to them.

Paul Dunn is head of *Results Accounting Systems*, an organisation that teaches business and marketing skills to accountants and their clients on three continents.

Dr Rich Madow is business advisor and the editor of the *Richards Report*, a highly regarded US based dental newsletter.

Dr Omar K. Reed is an internationally known speaker to dental professionals and head of the US *Pentegra* Group.

Mike Brasch is a cofounder of Federal Express who now teaches leadership through his company *Service Impact*.

Jay Abraham is a well-respected Californian marketing guru and head of *Abraham Publishing*.

Brad Sugars, a popular business speaker and author, is head of *Action International*, a company that specialises in marketing advice for business.

Ricardo Semler is an industrialist in Sao Paulo, Brazil and author of the extraordinary book, *Maverick*.

Chris Newton is chairman of the *Results Corporation* and author of 'The Do-it-Yourself Advertising Guide'.

Helen Parker is a partner in the UK based *Dental Business Solutions Group*.

Brian Sher heads *Vision Publishing,* a company that produces book summaries and seminars for people in business.

Philosophy ... from the Heart

Not every business book has such a depth of philosophy and simple wisdom. Paul has this to say of Paddi's story:

> As you read each page of this extraordinary book, you will come to know Paddi as a great philosopher – someone who's taken the most obvious of concepts and presented them in a way they've never been presented before. He's gone way beyond where most business people ever venture on their journey.

Chris this:

> Paddi was prepared to take risks in baring his soul ... This book will change the way that we all think about business ... open up new ways to create abundance in all its forms and to have fun growing older and happier. I hope you enjoy it as much as I have.

And Omer this:

> In the 1930's my father gave to me a checklist for business: it should be fun, profitable, win-win for all involved, have honesty and integrity at it's heart and do good for all mankind. Paddi has captured all this in his book.

And Paul believes Paddi is not just talking about business but about life:

> I bring to mind the words of a friend who died recently. Just two weeks before his death, he told me that our lives can be choreographed – that we can write the steps and the scripts, that we don't have to do things the 'traditional' way. Paddi brings that to life in this book. And he gives us the steps as well as the scripts.

Mike too:

> In the book, Paddi takes you back to what is truly important in life. Whenever I have a need to understand human nature, I ask Paddi Lund for his wisdom in its startling simplicity. Many times that wisdom is difficult to grasp but once mastered it becomes an indisputable aid to make your life more fulfilling, successful, and, dare I say it, joyful ...and your business goes through the roof!

Happiness-Centred ... but Practical!

Many people feel that happiness-in-business is just not practical. Here is what Rich feels about that theory:

> More important than price, location, marketing, or any of the other concepts that too many so-called experts freely discuss, happiness in the workplace is the basis for exemplary customer service, employee and owner satisfaction, and believe it or not ... profits!
>
> Could we focus on happiness, yet reap enormous profits? Could we have fun at work, yet operate more efficiently than ever? Could we avoid advertising altogether, yet generate more and better clients? The answers are yes, yes, and yes, and the reasons are explained within this timeless and fascinating book. Read 'Building the Happiness-Centred Business' – it very well could change your life too!

Chris agrees:

> When I first read the title I thought, "Happiness, what's that got to do with running a business? Isn't that a bit 'on the edge?'" But Paddi makes you think ... really think ... about having a happiness-centred business. Even more surprisingly he helps you understand that happiness in business isn't something you do instead of making money, but something that makes you money.
>
> Paddi's approach is a very down-to-earth, systematic

method for business happiness – something that, before
my eyes were opened, I would never have thought
achievable.

Paul also:

Paddi's built what to my mind is one of the most
astonishing businesses on the planet.

Paddi's given us a book as important as many of the
classically 'great business books'. But in here is not just
a business sense — it's life sense applied to business in a
unique and planned way. Not only that, this is not
theory. It actually damn well works! As you read,
you'll find yourself saying, 'Yes, that makes so much
sense'. Paddi's genius is that he's taken those 'sensible'
and obvious things that everyone else seems to have
missed and built them into a system.

And Brad, too:

I've recommended this book to literally thousands of
business owners for just one reason, so they'll understand
why people are so important, and how you can create an
environment where people not only want to work, but
want to excel. This book truly is an eye-opener.

Not Just for Dentists

Paul feels that Paddi's principles are universally
applicable to all business:

Yet as you'll discover, the fact that Paddi Lund earns his
living in a particular way is purely coincidental. You
see, in these pages Paddi redefines what it means to be
in business ... ANY business.

Mike has a similar view:

Paddi shows you in his book that it is not the big things
that are important in business. It is the little acts of
kindness that endear people to you. Now that isn't new

to people, on a personal level. What is news is that it works very effectively in business. In fact, when you fully grasp Paddi's simple business philosophies, it is difficult to understand why everyone doesn't conduct business the way he suggests. I have applied many of Paddi's principles with my clients in warehousing, manufacturing and hospital industries — they're charmingly simple ... and they work!

Jay too sees the book's usefulness across business boundaries:

If happiness, liberation, control and financial security are important to you, read this book. It will change the entire way you look at your life, business and value systems. A lot of people talk about paradigm shifting changing our belief systems, etc. But this man is the definitive expert on the subject.

Helen agrees:

This book should be required reading for all MBA students and indeed for anyone going into business. If people could apply Paddi's philosophy when they start out in business how much more fun and enjoyable their business lives would be. Paddi offers real hope for those who feel trapped with no way out.

And Brad:

Paddi's book is an insight into creating a business where everything is simple and yet so well thought out. Every step in Paddi's journey shows you how to grow a business where people matter ... a business designed to succeed into the 21st century.

As Rich says:

This book contains essential information that every business owner, professional, retail, service, or otherwise, needs to know. 'Building the Happiness-Centred Business' discusses a concept that not enough business owners understand, and that even fewer care to express. True happiness, however you define it, is at the heart of not just a fulfilling life, but a successful business, as well. Sadly, it is the only business book that I have ever read that contains such information.

A Pithy, but Immensely Readable Book!

If you have reached the stage in your life where you are looking for more than just sweat and tears from your business, and you like honesty and openness, you will find *Building the Happiness-Centred Business* is a hard book to put down. As Mike says:

> *This book is a rare treat. The story is one that needs to be trumpeted throughout the world. It is the only business book that I have read twice ... and continue to read.*

Paul has similar feelings:

> *You'll enjoy the style (even though it might seem strange at first — in a business book). You'll enjoy the simplicity, but most of all, you'll enjoy how you're able to take the many truths, the many insights and the examples and apply them in your business and life.*

And Rich:

> *This story by the remarkable Dr Paddi Lund is told with humour and warmth. It is one of the most wonderful books I have ever read.*

At first, Chris was taken in by the simplicity of Paddi's approach:

> *I really thought that I'd be able to skim this book. The truth is I started reading and got totally absorbed. I was taken with the understanding, the open style of writing, and the nice little unexpected twists that make reading this volume a pleasure. Paddi has a wonderful touch to the way he writes. Now I've been seduced into reading*

to the end of the book and I am late for the office. But it was worth it!

Ricardo, who is himself a great lateral thinker admires Paddi's unusual ideas and the results he achieved:

I liked this book very much and I found it full of innovating and new ways of looking at things. The more one can devise a differentiated point of view the more interesting and more efficient the solution.

Brad also appreciates Paddi's unusual style:

Take the worlds most painful business, add a dentist who is a little zany, and business principles that will revolutionise your life, and you've got this book. It's a journey into the way we all would be doing business … if only we thought of it first.

Well, what can I say after these sentiments? I hope you also enjoy Paddi's offering, and that it will help you to build your own version of the *Happiness-Centred* Business.

Fletcher Potanin, Publisher
For all at Solutions Press

BUSINESS IS NOT EASY!

For many years I felt inadequate because I found business very difficult. I thought that everyone else found it easy.

Business Is Not Easy!

For many years I felt inadequate because I found business very difficult. I thought that everyone else found it easy.

As a young man, unschooled in the world of commerce, and running a business for the first time, I was disagreeably surprised how difficult it all was. I thought that I must be doing something very wrong and that everyone else found business fairly simple: managed people easily, made money without a lot of effort and pursued their business in a calm and happy manner.

It was not until I had been toiling for a decade or so that I had time to draw breath and look around with a more mature and inquiring eye. It was then I saw that what I had believed to be true about the majority of businesses — that they ran smoothly and with little effort — was not in reality how things were.

Business is hard, and people often find that their work is stressful, unfulfilling emotionally and doesn't return the financial rewards they feel they deserve for their efforts. For many, business is the most difficult thing in life, and work worries occupy a great part of their waking thoughts.

Each year a large number of people kill themselves because of business worries. Some people spend so much time, effort and attention on their business that their marriages break up and their children grow up without enough love. Others die or become sick because of stress induced disease caused by business worry.

When I discovered that I was not alone in my difficulties with running a business, I didn't feel so isolated and stupid. That was certainly a relief and, freed of guilt, I could now look at my business in a more positive, problem-solving way.

Business is certainly not easy, it's true, and yet, paradoxically, business can provide us with some of our greatest pleasures. To feel truly fulfilled and happy in our lives most of us seem to need the structure and challenge that our work provides. We need complex problems to solve and we need to feel that we are accomplishing something useful. For me the pleasure of solving a difficult business puzzle or making an effective but complex management decision is as good or better than any other intellectual pleasure in my life.

BOOKS, GURUS, ADVICE & MISTAKES

In an effort to improve my own business acumen I read many books and listened to a lot of advice. There were, and still are, certainly a plethora of books written about business and an abundance of gurus to tell us how to do business better. Sometimes these authors and advisers give us very useful advice. Often that advice is good but not very applicable to our business needs, and sometimes we feel that the advice is not useful at all — for anyone.

I think that no one can really tell you all of the things you need to achieve success and happiness in your own business — sometimes you have to make and learn from your own mistakes.

My book is a story about mistakes — making them and learning from them. If there is one thing I have learned from all my business heartache and trials, it is that the greatest sin is to give up, or become paralysed with the fear of making mistakes.

As I look back I find that the successes were as much due to learning from failures as to the occasional great flashes of inspiration. Often the pain and suffering after a failure indicates that the price has been paid and now is the time to expect the rewards. Just keep going that extra few steps, put in one more little bit of effort, and it will fly.

HAPPINESS FOCUSED

For many years the focus of my business aspirations has been to have the pleasure of challenge from business without having to put up with damaging stress. By developing a **Happiness-Centred Business** I have learnt that it is possible — possible to enjoy business. I can make a healthy profit and one day die feeling that all the effort and time spent in my business world has not been time wasted, but has been an integral, important fulfilling element in my life.

Happiness-Centred Business is about being focused on achieving happiness above all else.

Our natural impulse is to focus on our happiness, but we often work unhappily because we see no other way. We then try to buy some of the happiness on which we missed out with the money we have earned.

I find it much more efficient and pleasant to have enough happiness at work, so that I don't have to spend my time scrambling after it in my private life.

Being happiness-focused does not mean a decrease in profits, in fact it means just the opposite. It is a means for profit increase. (However, whether or not the profit does increase becomes less important when you are happy!)

Most business is money focused. The focus on money makes it much harder to avoid the destructive stresses. What does it avail us when we make a lot of money, if our health is compromised, if we die young, if we lose the respect of our children and spouses?

Many people in management positions are unhappy, overweight, caffeine addicted, lacking exercise and heading for an early grave. I think that the focus on money often leads people to ignore their bodies and spirits. When money is the focus human beings assume a lesser significance. Even one's own body and emotional well being become less important than the almighty dollar.

I think that running a business is a lot like riding a bicycle. It's only when you give up trying so hard to balance that the task becomes natural. In business, profit comes more easily when the business is full of happy people making their customers happy, than when everyone is focused solely on the Bottom Line.

No, I am not saying that all we need to do to make a good profit is to focus on happiness! To run a profitable business we still need the systems and principles that have been developing as long as there has been commerce and industry — effective management, a sense of common purpose, a pleasant environment in which to work and efficient business systems. What I do say is that focusing on happiness makes profitability easier and it gives us an amazing gift — more happiness from our businesses and in our lives.

AWESOME CUSTOMER SERVICE

The most carefully crafted and well meant mission statements will not motivate the business team members to provide Awesome Service unless they can see some benefit to themselves in providing such service.

AWESOME CUSTOMER SERVICE

The most carefully crafted and well meant mission statements will not motivate the business team members to provide Awesome Service unless they can see some benefit to themselves in providing such service.

few years ago my business-family and I were heavily featured in a training video called *Towards Awesome Service.*

The video sold well and I received much positive feedback from people who had purchased it. They were impressed with the level of service that we provided to our customers and set out to do the same in their own businesses.

After a few months many were still having problems getting the ideas off the ground. They had written the mission statements. They had made the manuals. They themselves had the vision. They knew they wanted their staff to provide Awesome Service to their customers, but they found their staff were not performing to their expectations.

I have seen manuals and mission statements from many businesses.

They describe in detail how wonderful their service will be:

Each member of the organisation will constantly strive to satisfy the customer!

We earnestly believe that the customer is the most important person in our organisation!

In our business the customer will always be right.

These are noble aspirations, but too often in the past statements like these have been from businesses that provided the worst service; with the result that mission statements have come to be regarded indifferently or downright cynically by many staff members.

I think it is important to realise that the old adage 'you can lead a horse to water, but you cannot make him drink' is still true today. To be effectively motivated **everyone needs a good, selfish reason for their actions.**

Customers don't buy from anyone unless they see benefits to themselves. Business owners don't run a business if there is no profit. Why should we think that the principles of motivation work any differently for the people in the business team?

 THE MOST CAREFULLY CRAFTED AND WELL-MEANT MISSION STATEMENTS WILL NOT MOTIVATE PEOPLE TO PROVIDE GREAT SERVICE UNLESS THEY CAN SEE SOME BENEFIT TO THEMSELVES IN PROVIDING SUCH SERVICE.

No matter what it says in the manual or the mission statement, if they are left to act independently, front line people will do the things that they see will benefit themselves. If they see benefits in serving customers well they will do it, but if they don't see the advantage to themselves they won't.

The perceived benefits that lead people to acts of great service can be many. They can be financial, intellectual or the avoidance of punishment, but those acts motivated by emotional rewards are most consistently performed.

 THE MOST EFFECTIVE MOTIVATOR FOR PROVIDING GREAT SERVICE IS A SINCERE INTEREST AND CARE FOR THE PERSON YOU ARE SERVING.

An added benefit of having the acts motivated by a perceived emotional reward is that they are more warmly regarded by customers. Think about it. Would you rather have a smile from someone who is acting from fear of punishment or a smile from someone because they are earnestly concerned for your happiness? I suspect you would prefer the latter, and I think you would be perceptive enough to tell one from the other. Your customers probably think and feel the same!

There is no way that I know of that will force someone in your business-family to care about customers, but you can make the business framework such that caring for customers becomes natural. Systems set up to achieve great service, but which do not address the emotional aspects of service, usually, do not work.

You can force people to say things that are designed to show 'caring for the customer', but forced, insincere greetings and expressions of interest are easy to spot.

For me, I prefer poor service to a parody of caring.

The Checkout Operator

Checkout operators often ask me, "How are you today?" Almost invariably they ask without looking at me or waiting for an answer. For me this is a negative emotional experience. The first time I was asked I was even silly enough to answer the question and disclose how I was. It was really quite embarrassing. I suddenly realised that an answer was not needed — she did not care how I felt. My words hung in the air conspicuous in their redundancy and I was embarrassed.

It seems to me that most checkout operators must be instructed to ask that question, "How are you today?" Perhaps it is in an operations manual somewhere. However, looking directly at the customer as the question is asked and waiting for the answer does not seem to be part of the system.

IS THERE A BETTER WAY?

It would be interesting if checkout operators were given enough instruction in the niceties of politeness to make the greeting a happy experience for them and the customer. Even if at first the operator didn't care much for the customer, things could change.

Perhaps the checkout operator would see the flicker of pleasure in the eye of the customer who enjoyed the warm greeting, and gain pleasure from having created happiness in another person. An action which was at first mechanical, might then become self perpetuating and sincere.

Perhaps the checkout operator would greet a co-worker with the same eye contact and sincerity.

Perhaps the store would become a happier place for customers and for the people who worked in it.

Perhaps the surrounding community would become a better place in which to live because it had such a happy store.

Perhaps the store would prosper and the world would become a happier, more affluent place for you and I ...

I think it would.

I don't believe that my checkout operator was an uncaring person. I feel she would have acted differently if she knew the joy of giving pleasure to her customers. I am sure if she had given her customers a warm greeting on their previous visit, they would have chosen to use her check-out rather than any of the other operators. She and her customers would have felt pleasure from mutual recognition and rewarding social contact. What kept her and her customers from this pleasure was the culture of the organisation in which she was employed.

I firmly believe that it is possible to implant and nurture a culture of politeness and warmth into a business, so that after the initial mechanical efforts the emotional rewards are enough to ensure that it continues, self-fuelled.

But how can we start off this process?

For my team and me, the basis of our ability to provide what others have called 'awesome service', is a system for human interaction and communication that we have collected from many sources and developed over a number of years. It is called the 'Courtesy System'.

COURTESY SYSTEM

Unless people are happy within themselves, it is hard for them to be consistently pleasant to those whom they serve.

If you are working in an unhappy atmosphere with people you do not like it takes tremendous effort to care for customers ... and customers can detect the ersatz. A smile pasted on an unhappy face or ostensibly 'awesome service' from someone preoccupied with their own problems are seen for what they are: a parody of caring.

The Courtesy System, which I will describe a little later, is about providing the motivation that helps everyone to **enjoy** giving wonderful service. It is a system designed to improve politeness and to generate communication and interpersonal skills that everyone in the business-family can use to become happy at work.

There is no 'quick fix' way to great service. The motivation needs to come from deep within.

 TO CONSISTENTLY PROVIDE WONDERFUL CUSTOMER SERVICE, IT IS IMPORTANT TO CHANGE THE SPIRIT IN THE ORGANISATION, NOT JUST THE OPERATING MANUAL.

Initially the Courtesy System produces a similar result to that seen in my checkout operator — people are polite without much warmth. But gradually, as the team members get positive feedback from those to whom they are polite, the interaction becomes natural and caring.

For me to tell you that politeness is the key to happiness and customer service seems too simplistic, so, if you will allow me, I will take you on the journey that led me to this point of view.

The Man with the Smile

One day as I drove to work I saw a young man who was also on his way to work. He was dressed in green overalls and was walking towards a sheltered workshop where I surmised he had a job with the garden maintenance crew. By his unusual appearance, I surmised he had Down's Syndrome. But what struck me most about him was not his unusual features or gait, but that he was smiling.

He was going to work, and he was smiling!

As I continued on my journey I looked carefully, but could not see a smile on the face of any other person in the morning rush. It seemed to me that, except for the man in the green overalls, no one was looking forward to their work. Could it be that everybody was less happy in their jobs than the young man with the smile? I'm sure we commuters all made more money in a week than he was likely to do. I'm sure that we all had a greater understanding of business principles than he had. But still, the boy in the green overalls seemed happier than any other person I saw on my journey that morning. Thinking deeply as I drove along, weighed down with the thought that perhaps the burden of intelligence is unhappiness, I eventually came to the conclusion that mentality is not a barrier to happiness ... it merely makes it more difficult to achieve. The more intellectual we are, the more distractions we have to take us from sensible goals and the more effort and thought we have to put into achieving that most sensible of goals — happiness.

It was not at that point that I saw the need to create a system to give me happiness at my work ... but it was when the idea was first germinated.

Insanity —
A Catalyst
for Change

This is my journey through the outer fringes of
sanity. I tell you about my experience of
madness in gory detail.

Insanity — A Catalyst for Change

This is my journey through the outer fringes of sanity. I tell you about my experience of madness in gory detail.

I had been experiencing an assortment of unpleasant feelings for about two weeks. I can remember having many of the symptoms about which I had read in dusty textbooks of psychiatry — books written by men with strange sounding Germanic names that I had glimpsed in the depths of the Medical Library stacks.

I heard voices.

I saw visions.

I felt that others could read my thoughts and were judging me as unfit to live in normal society.

I felt persecuted.

I was obsessive and compulsive about my obsessions.

For a few minutes, I was God.

Strange Symptoms

It was strange that each set of symptoms lasted for such a short time. For a few minutes, I felt that my lover Debra knew all the answers to life and she would tell me and lead me into the light. My voices were with me for a day or two at most. One day, during a whole lunchtime I struggled to lock the office door. I locked it and checked it and returned to check that I had locked it, only to return again and again to check that I had checked that I had locked it again. I can still feel myself on my hands and knees crawling towards the door trying to stop myself from inspecting the lock one last time. I remember being deeply afraid that someone would see me and know what I had become — mad!

Eventually, one afternoon, I came to a turning point from which I would either return to normality, or fall deeper into madness.

The Turning Point

Somewhere inside my brain lies recorded the whole of the experience, but I can only see glimpses of it, like flashes of light off the water seen through trees at the bottom of my garden.

It was a hot day. The quality of the light makes me think it must have been summer. I was lying on my bed and people were talking in the lounge room next door. Even when my thoughts became really scary for me, I was still sufficiently aware that because there were people close by I should not cry out and disturb them. I was deadly afraid of what would happen if they found out what I was thinking and how strange, convoluted and crazed my thoughts had become. I can remember the dull feeling of anxiety pain in my stomach, not so severe as appendicitis, but somehow worse because it was not a clean pain. Not like a wound, more like having a cage of rats resting on my stomach, gnawing at me. It was not only a physical pain, but also a pain of my spirit.

Suddenly a white light descended and enfolded me and with it came a wonderful peace of mind. A man's voice spoke to me. I felt a calm I had never felt before. I can't remember what he said, and I didn't see him clearly. As the light and the voice faded I can remember thinking 'I thought it would be more perfect.' It didn't seem that the light had been absolutely white, or the man perfectly good, or the voice perfectly reassuring. I felt guilty and furtive thinking such blasphemy.

Like a punishment for such bad thoughts, I was suddenly surrounded by a deep blackness. Then I heard another voice, cold and sinister. Again, I have forgotten the words, but I can remember the awful fear the words gave to me. The owner of the voice led me to the place at the centre of me. I found I was looking into an endlessly deep pit and I was very afraid. As quickly as it came, the darkness receded, the voice fell silent and I was left feeling drained.

I had been taking Valium for the previous two weeks to help me sleep and I found myself in the bathroom with a tablet in my hand. I felt a little stronger holding in my hand the means for temporary escape. As I started to raise the tablet to my mouth the voice of the darkness returned and told me that if I took the tablet I would be damned forever and I would fall, or be pushed into the bottomless hole that lay at the centre of my soul. I stood looking into the mirror. I saw myself looking overwhelmingly haggard and in a detached way, I felt sorry for myself as one would for another human in dire distress. I popped the pill and, almost instantly, fell into a deep sleep.

When I awoke I felt a little better and over the next three days I became more and more my old self. On the fourth day I gave up the Valium, slept deeply and naturally the whole night and well into the morning and woke refreshed and alert. I felt as though I had passed through a long dark tunnel. I remember feeling the words 'Baptism By Fire' were appropriate but the flames must have been cold and dark. I could now see the light at the end of the tunnel — light that I had not seen for a long time. It shone on me and warmed my bones.

SYSTEM FOR SANITY

Throughout my brief sojourn with insanity I had kept a degree of introspection.

In my lucid times I would write notes to the 'me' of the dark times; little practical hints to help me to return from 'the pit'.

Don't think too deeply about what you are thinking about.

(Because if you think about what you are thinking about and you are thinking about what you are thinking, you'll soon find yourself falling into a black hole which is like a whirlpool where your thoughts go round and round and round.)

Don't tell people what you are feeling.

(Or they will lock you up and if they do you will never get free, because they will treat you as insane and pretty soon you will be insane; all of the time; forever.)

These notes to myself helped me to recover my sanity.

As I thought about it afterwards, I discovered that I had been developing a system to help my recovery. If I can come from madness to sanity with the help of a system, I wondered to myself, can a system also take me from unhappiness to happiness?

I Make a Discovery

Because I had endured and recovered from my madness I became stronger.

That which does not kill you will make you strong.

Because I became stronger, I could look at things in my life and work that before I had been afraid to examine too closely.

I now can face my period of madness and be thankful for the lessons it taught me. I know I have the seeds of madness in me, maybe we all do, but now I know what it was that watered and nurtured those seeds.

It was my job.

HAPPINESS METER

I discover that 'happiness' is important. I make a tool to measure it and discover a little about how to have more of it.

The Happiness Meter

The Dentist's happiness
level starts to increase.

Illustrated by
Brian Doyle

Happiness Meter

*I discover that 'happiness' is important. I
make a tool to measure it and discover a little
about how to have more of it.*

did not enjoy my period of insanity and did
not want to go through it again. But my
experience did give me the strength and a
compelling reason to re-examine my life.

I began to realise that my insanity was an attempt to
escape from an unpleasant existence. I was relatively
happy at home, but at work I was deeply unhappy.
Much of my job I did not enjoy at all.

Like many people I defined myself and my worth in
terms of my job. If I failed in my vocation I would be a
failure at life. This is a big pressure.

I was reasonably successful, financially independent
and respected by my patients and friends, but I had
paid a heavy price for that success.

I made money from my work and received respect, but
I didn't get much love there — I didn't even realise I
needed any. Later on I discovered that I was far from
alone in feeling this way.

MOST PEOPLE CANNOT BE HAPPY WHERE THEY
DO NOT FEEL LOVED.

I AM A DENTIST

People hate dentists! If you thought that dentists
deserve to go insane, you would not be alone!

Many people dislike lawyers, but reserve their deepest
repugnance for the dental profession. Often they like
their own dentist, but still hate dentists in general. I
don't think most dentists realise that it is possible to
hate a group and yet like an individual. I certainly
didn't understand this concept.

The most common opinion about dentists that dentists
hear from their clients is, **"I really hate dentists**!" This
is often followed by the apology. "Oh, not you, of
course, just dentists in general." But it's too late. The
barb has penetrated.

> *They say they hate dentists, so they must mean just
> that ... they hate dentists ...I am a dentist ... so they
> must hate me!*

Maybe they have good cause to hate. I know that
dentists are not renowned for their sensitivity. (Attila
the Hun featured in at least two dental jokes I have
heard.)

Are we dentists born insensitive, trained to it, or do we
just become that way because everyone says nasty
things about us and we come to hate our jobs? I think
the latter.

It seems to me that the souls of dentists often shrivel up and die for lack of love and attention.

One Way to Leave an Un-Rewarding Job – For Good!

Many dentists have an interesting way of dealing with the difficulties of their profession — they kill themselves.

In western civilisations, dentists are often in the professional employment category most active in suicide. They commit suicide at a far greater rate than that of the population average.

It's interesting to think about what it means when people commit suicide. What they are saying to the world is 'I would rather be dead than alive.' Bearing in mind that for most people death is the 'Great Unknown' and that the unknown is very frightening, the life of someone who commits suicide must not have been very pleasant.

It was worrying for me being in a profession where I felt it was almost expected that one would take one's own life in this way. It was rather like standing on the edge of a yawning chasm, or on the parapet of a very tall building. You know that you don't want to jump, but something is pulling you towards the edge and you lean over a little further and further, until whoops, suddenly you are over the edge in free flight, seeing your life in vivid Technicolor.

I remember I had even taped to the reception desk a magazine article titled 'High Incidence of Suicide among Dentists'. I suppose I was hoping everyone would be nice to me out of sympathy.

LIFE IN A DENTAL OFFICE

Please let me tell you what it is like to be a dentist.

It's not easy spending all day doing things with sharp, rapidly rotating instruments inside the sensitive, dark, moist mouths of people — people who would really rather be somewhere else, doing something else: anything else.

An improbable conversation:

> *Nothing to do tonight! Maybe we could go to the cinema? … What about a walk by the river to watch the sunset? … Oh, I know … let's go down to Dr. L's and have some Root Canal work done!*

If I describe how it was in my practice six or seven years ago, it will give you an idea of what life still is like for some dentists.

Time was planned to the nearest second. Patients scheduled for 48 hours of the week, each moment accounted for. By using time and motion studies, output was maximised. The business ran like a production line for Swiss watches: fine tuned, precise and delicate.

But somehow something always managed to screw up the delicate balance. A patient came fifteen minutes late and messed up the schedule. Someone had a toothache and had to be fitted in in spite of the fact that there was no time. Fitting a bridge took twice as long at it was meant to.

Crisis to Crisis

Time: Tues. 23/4/85. 4 pm.
Place: The PGL Dental Emporium.
Three patients are pacing on the Axminster-carpet in the waiting room.

We (*the team*) start to snap at each other. The tension rises. Because I am tense I am not as gentle as I can be and the patient has some pain. Fearfully, the patient guards his teeth with his tongue and cheek muscles so the work progresses more slowly. My fingers become fatigued as I push harder to hold away the defending tongue so that I can see the teeth. My whole arm starts to ache.

I mumble a request for another instrument, a request which Pat, the dental nurse, doesn't hear. (*Can't she hear what I am saying? Isn't she listening to me? Why is she thinking of other things while I sweat?*) I repeat the request more loudly and a touch of irritation creeps into my voice. Annoyed, Pat slaps the instrument into my hand. Anger flares from all sides and simmers for the rest of the day.

If things became really stressful and I felt unappreciated I would do a 'prima donna'. This little act showed my co-workers that they should appreciate me more. (*Well at least that's what I thought it did. In reality it just made them think I was stupid and egotistical.*)

Without consciously admitting my intention I increase the stress and tension, until eventually someone makes an error because the pressure has become intolerable. This gives me the excuse I need to justify blowing my top, releases my tension, and makes everyone realise that I am doing a very difficult job. I am a hero who performs successfully ... even when surrounded by incompetence. When I make their life difficult, the longsuffering staff have their own little ways to get back at me and make me suffer:

silent martyrdom … subtle back-stabbing … quiet sabotage. And so we continue through the day, lurching from crisis to crisis, playing nasty little games … offensive game … defensive game. Finally we leave the office sweating and trembling.

At home we dissipate the stress as best we can, by drinking it away, or transferring it onto the shoulders of our families. (*Families are meant to share things, aren't they?*)

COPING WITH DENTAL STRESS

Dental nurses traditionally cope with their difficult environment by moving from dentist to dentist in an effort to find a pleasant situation. (From talking with dentists and their nurses, I learnt that the industry average seems to be about nine months stay in each job before moving on. This is very wasteful of everyone's time in retraining and developing new relationships.)

Eventually many dental nurses leave their profession while still young and do something less stressful so then there are too few older and experienced dental nurses.

Dentists have invested far more in their education, so it is difficult for them to make the decision to change their occupation. They cope in different ways.

A few become insane or alcoholic.

Some do leave the profession to take up other vocations such as property developing or oyster farming.

Some become unfeeling and set up great barriers to interpersonal contact so that the stress can't get to them. They kill themselves emotionally.

Some kill themselves literally.

And some devise ways of pursuing their occupation happily and successfully.

I decided I would learn to enjoy my work. I had invested too much time and effort in learning my skills to give them up. I have thankfully joined that happy last group and I plan to spend the rest of my life being a happy dentist!

GOALS AND MEASUREMENT

I often address groups of accountants. I talk about life in general, Systems for Business and Systems for Happiness.

Accountants are not as boring and staid as everyone thinks and, like dentists, they often feel trapped in their professionalism and find it hard to relate to their clients. Once they catch a new vision for business they are surprisingly quick to change.

I find there is a sort of reverse osmosis when I talk with people. I end up absorbing at least as much from them as they do from me and my work with accountants has allowed me to gain some knowledge of their work.

Understandably, because of their profession, accountants are usually very focused on money. They are used to setting financial goals for themselves and their clients. The most popular homily used by the accounting profession has to be 'If you set a goal, you will reach it!'

At any time, accountants can tell how you are going in relation to your financial goal by counting up how much money you have made compared with how much you want. They have Benchmarks, Graphs and Cash Flow Charts, all designed to let their clients know whether or not they are on target to achieve their financial goals.

HAPPINESS AT WORK?

My goal became *Happiness at work.*

The question I had to answer was, "How do you measure happiness?"

Accountants seem to have no problem measuring money, they just count it! My problem was I couldn't think how to count happiness.

I did know that my emotional state varied between happy and unhappy, so I thought it would be useful to devise a way to record both the unhappiness and the happiness, just as accountants do the debits and credits with their red and black ink.

Unhappiness I felt was the same as 'stress' and, because I felt it was easier to sense my stress than my unhappiness, it was 'stress' that I decided to measure.

In retrospect, I feel that equating stress to unhappiness was not quite correct. Stress does not automatically lead to unhappiness and, in fact, we all need a certain amount of stress to stop us from becoming bored. At that time, however, our work team had so much stress and it was so intimately related to our unhappiness, that it was as though they were the same. I seemed to be used to acknowledging if I was 'Stressed Out', but not if I was 'unhappy'. Anyway right or wrong, it was 'happiness' and 'stress' that I settled on as the 'Debits' and 'Credits'.

Another thing that struck me was that my happiness was intimately tied up with that of the other members of the team with whom I worked. When they were happy I was usually happy. When they were unhappy it was hard for me to be happy. Therefore, I thought it would be a good idea if we did the measurement as a group so that we could all see each other's happiness level.

With these thoughts in mind I invented the Happiness Meter.

A TOOL TO MEASURE HAPPINESS

For all its complicated sounding name, in the end I produced what was quite a simple tool. The Happiness Meter was a laminated chart on which the names of the team members were inscribed. There was a squared vertical grid on which we placed counters that indicated our score.

The 'Meter' sat on the wall where we could all see it and be mindful of our happiness or stress of the previous day.

Every day, at the end of the day, we would meet together as a group and sit around the meter.

Each of us would take a turn being the facilitator — the person responsible for asking questions about our happiness and recording them on the meter. A session would go on as follows:

FACIL   Paddi, on a scale of 1 to 10, how much happiness have you had today?

I would reply (typically) – "2 or 3".

The facilitator would then calibrate the Happiness Meter.

FACIL   Paddi, on a scale of 1 to 10, how much stress have you had today?

PADDI   7 or 8. (*Or 12 on a bad day!*)

> *The facilitator again calibrates the Happiness*
> *Meter. Each member of the team would, in their*
> *turn, be asked the same questions. At that time,*
> *our scores were invariably similar: 0 to 4 for*
> *Happiness and 6 to 10 for Stress.*

After the first weeks the scores seemed to improve. Then we discovered we were all exaggerating our happiness scores. We had thought it would make everyone else feel better if they felt we were happy.

We discussed this and decided that this didn't help and it would be better to be truthful.

Scores improved a little, but not much. We could measure the degree of happiness that we experienced, but we didn't seem to be able to do much to change it.

CONTROL

The more I thought about happiness, unhappiness and stress, the more I was able to stand back from myself and observe how I reacted when something started to become stressful for me.

I found that there was always a point where I decided to be emotionally affected by whatever it was that was happening — in effect to surrender to my negative emotions. Feeling 'stressed out' and 'unhappy' was not just something that happened to me. I was in control of my mind and emotions and it was I who decided whether or not to become stressed and unhappy.

This discovery made me feel more in control of myself, but I did realise that there were certainly things that happened that made it more difficult not to respond stressfully and sometimes, as with the 'Prima Donna' reaction, I recognised that I deliberately engineered situations to increase my own stress.

After I shared my thoughts with the others, we decided not to talk about being 'stressed out' but instead to say 'doing stress' to emphasise the fact that we had a choice.

DOING STRESS

There is an expression that goes 'Let's do breakfast'. I first heard it in a movie set in California — 'LA Story' I think.

'Doing breakfast' imbues the expectation of the meal with the idea of a 'power meal', an occasion where things of import will be discussed. The meal will not just happen and pass by unnoticed, it will be performed purposefully for a reason greater than that of just ingesting for nutrition.

When we began to see the dynamics of stress, we came to appreciate the largely volitional and purposeful nature that it has. Like the 'power meal', our reaction to stress was often a performance ... for a purpose.

We had a purpose in losing control. We were not always consciously aware that we had, but, as we examined our motives more closely, we discovered that it was almost always there.

Sometimes the purpose of 'doing' the stress was to show others that we were overworked, sometimes it meant that we were not getting enough attention, and sometimes it indicated that we felt that the way we were being treated belied our importance.

There are always stresses in our environment, but we have the freedom of choice whether or not to 'do stress' ... and whether or not we do stress usually depends on the effect we are looking to achieve.

We can have stress, just as we have a normal breakfast: take the useful nutritional things and eliminate those things that are not useful. Or we can 'do' the stress like a power meal — make it into a performance to validate our actions, appease our unhappiness and control others around us.

Calling the game 'doing stress' made it obvious how childish and actively or passively aggressive the behaviour was. How silly to choose to give oneself pain to 'show off' and control others — to lose control in an effort to gain control.

Doing stress, regardless of one's position in the business team, was seen and named for what it was — an undesirable and unproductive power game, damaging to all parties involved.

DISCLOSING OUR FEELINGS

I shared my thoughts about 'doing stress' with the others. At the next meeting, each member of the team began to disclose more of their personal feelings about the things that were causing their stress.

These disclosures helped to uncover the reasons why we felt stressed and unhappy during that day.

At the Happiness meeting:

FACIL   Jenny, on a scale of 1 to 10, how much unhappiness do you feel you have had today?

JENNY   10 (*1 2 3 4 5 6 7 8 9 10 — very unhappy*)

FACIL   Jenny, what was it that caused your unhappiness?

JENNY   He told me to pass something and then he grabbed it from me as if he thought I had been too slow.

or

JENNY   She made me mad. She raised her voice to me.

or

JENNY   You didn't even say 'thank you' when I went out of my way to help you.

What made us most unhappy, it became apparent, were the little forgotten courtesies and the unkind or thoughtless words or actions.

 MOST UNHAPPINESS WAS NOT RELATED TO THE AMOUNT OF MONEY THAT WE MADE FOR THE DAY, OR THE PACE OF THE WORK: IT WAS LARGELY DETERMINED BY HOW WE TREATED EACH OTHER.

THE POWER OF DISCOURTESY

One day Merilyn, one of the nurses, resigned her job. The reason she gave was that I had spoken to her impolitely.

I could remember the incident that had upset her, but it seemed to me that I had just talked to her normally. Probably I had been talking 'normally' to her for a long time. To Merilyn my normal way of speaking was impolite and it caused an accumulation of bad feelings that peaked at that last perceived discourtesy. She felt she couldn't stay with me any longer.

After missing her greatly, I decided I would have to apologise. I said how sorry I was and that cleared the air enormously. She returned back to the fold.

I can remember thinking,

*I don't really know why I should be apologising. I
don't think I said very unpleasant things to her. Surely
just the words that I used couldn't make her want to
leave a good job?*

As I later came to realise they could and did!

I started to ponder on politeness,

*Could it be that impolite words are powerful enough
to make someone want to leave a good job? Perhaps
the unhappiness and stress that we are having is
largely caused by lack of politeness.*

*Will we solve our problems if we make some
standards of behaviour that ensure everyone is treated
with courtesy and politeness?*

Why don't we try it?

So we met together and we designed a 'performance
standard' to regulate courtesy and politeness.

It was:

---

*Use 'Please' and 'Thank you' whenever you ask
for or receive something.*

(This rule evolved into Performance Standard 1 in the
present Courtesy System.)

We placed this Performance Standard on the notice
board and everyone tried to apply it.

We started to notice an improvement in our happiness.

The change was slow at first. But gradually, each day
we were reporting more 'happiness' and less
'unhappiness'.

Encouraged, we thought of a second Performance Standard.

It was:

If you have a problem with someone, talk to them about it and no one else.

(This rule evolved into Performance Standards 2 and 3 in the present Courtesy System.)

After using these two rules for a few months we were typically reporting 8 and 9 for 'Happiness' and 1 and 2 for 'Unhappiness/Stress'.

The change was not easy, change never is, but the rewards were great enough to keep us going. Slowly we were reaching the stage where good days had become common and life was becoming better for us all. We still did have occasional bad days, but because of our successes they made us try harder rather than discouraging us.

We had devised a Courtesy System which later would become part of the framework for our new 'Happiness-Centred' Business.

CAN A HAPPY BUSINESS MAKE MONEY?

I discover I had sacrificed happiness, to earn money … that bought less happiness than I had sacrificed.

Can a Happy Business Make Money?

I discover I had sacrificed happiness, to earn money … that bought less happiness than I had sacrificed.

---

didn't learn much about running a business in Dental School and when I graduated in 1969, after nearly six years of relative poverty, money was not very important to me. I was poor, but happy.

Friday Night on the Town

I remember the highlight of my week was to go to a North Adelaide hamburger shop on a Friday evening.

I would sit in a corner and, with great relish, consume chips and a typical Australian hamburger (thick and juicy with onions, beetroot, salad, egg and cheese), eating from the newspaper in which they came wrapped. I can still remember the taste — few meals today come close to it. It was romantic to be sitting in the fuggy, greasy atmosphere, drinking Coke, television blaring, watching the passers by. Most of the week I lived on chocolate and apples and the occasional meal I could filch from the mothers of young ladies of my acquaintance. I remember one of them (a mother that is) christened me 'Paddi the Parasite' because of my habit of arriving at meal times and departing soon after ... clutching leftovers. I also remember that I didn't much care what she called me, so long as I had eaten well. Life was not easy, but it was simple. Stress came (at meal times) but it was not constant. I WAS HAPPY!

When I finally graduated, I was paid 100 dollars for a weeks' work. A king's ransom, compared with what I'd had! It was an embarrassment. I didn't know how to spend that much. For the first few months I lived on about one twentieth of it and hoped the rest would somehow disappear from my bank account so that I didn't have to concern myself with it. I could never conceive of spending so much money. How much worse things were to become over the next ten years — I became a successful dentist.

At age 35 I had plenty of money but it seemed to disappear as fast as I made it. I spent lavishly on the things I knew would help me to feel fulfilled, but I never quite seemed to have enough to buy that ultimate illusory thing that would finally give me happiness. I became convinced that I had to become richer, so I learned more about business from books and my peers. I learned that the only way to earn more was to be absolutely focused on money. I became single-minded in that direction and I succeeded. I became a very financially successful dentist.

I could buy most things that took my fancy. Yet I found myself increasingly unhappy as I worked longer and harder to buy more and more in a vain attempt to obtain some happiness for myself. I felt I should work even harder to make more money ... I became stressed and unhappy ... I bought more things to try to get a little happiness ... I had to work harder to earn more money to pay for these new things. And so it went on, around and around the financial merry-go-round.

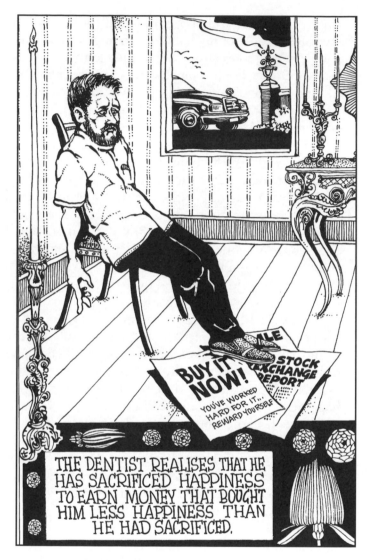

THE DENTIST REALISES THAT HE HAS SACRIFICED HAPPINESS TO EARN MONEY THAT BOUGHT HIM LESS HAPPINESS THAN HE HAD SACRIFICED.

The Money-Centred Busines

The Dentist realises that he has sacrificed happiness to earn money that bought him less happiness than he had sacrificed.

Illustrated by
Brian Doyle

Looking back on my experiences, this idea: 'to make money is the most important thing', proved to be the concept that led me furthest from happiness.

HAPPINESS OR MONEY?

Many people feel that having happiness at work is not consistent with making a profit.

Some years later, at a business seminar, I was speaking to a group of people, extolling the virtues and advantages of working towards happiness in business.

I thought I had done quite well. They stayed in their seats, laughed in the right places and gave me a good round of applause. I was a little taken aback by the first question from John E, who was an accountant.

JOHN E Yes I understand all you are saying about getting more happiness at work and I think its wonderful that you and your team have so much pleasure in your work ... but how can you make any money when you are spending all your time enjoying yourselves?

Judging by the audience's reaction, he asked what was obviously on the minds of many.

Here is my guess at the dialogue that was occurring in John's brain just before he asked that question.

Everyone knows that we go to work for money, don't they? Yes of course they do! And you can't enjoy yourself if you are working hard trying to make money, can you? No, of course not, work's too stressful. So this Paddi guy is either a charlatan, or an idiot … or he's crazy.

But I don't want to seem rude … so I'll ask him a question that will bring out the truth of the matter.

"How can you make any money when you are spending all your time enjoying yourselves?"

Luckily I had pondered this sort of question before and over the years I had made some interesting self-discoveries about happiness and the reasons why I wanted to earn money.

WHY DO YOU WANT TO EARN MONEY?

Ten years ago you could have had the following conversation with me.

YOU   Paddi, why do you go to work?

ME   Because I get fulfilment from it and I like people.

YOU   Would you go to work if you didn't make any money?

ME   (*After some thought*) No.

YOU   So the money is more important to you than the other factors?

ME   Yes, I suppose you are right.

YOU   Paddi, why do you want the money?

ME   To buy 'things'.

YOU   Why do you want to buy 'things?

ME   Because they make me feel good.

YOU   Why do you want to feel good?

ME   Because that is what I want to do with my life
— to spend my time feeling good (*being
happy*).

YOU   So you want money to buy a little happiness?

ME   … Yes, I suppose so.

I have purposely made this conversation a little
simplistic because I feel that I must have been simple
minded to act as I did. I am annoyed at myself for
wasting so much of my life in unhappiness, stupidly
believing that money would buy me more happiness
than I had given up.

MICHELLE AND GOALS

Not long after we had started using the Courtesy
System and happiness levels had been improving, I had
a conversation with Michelle. Michelle is one of the
Care Nurses and was aged nineteen at the time.

I was trying to find out if she understood that the
improvement in our happiness was related to the new
systems we had set in place.

Michelle is an incorrigible prankster and I should have
known better than to have expected a straight answer
from her, but she did demonstrate that she understood
very well — perhaps better than I did.

PADDI   I've noticed that everyone seems to be a lot
happier lately.

MICH   Yes, I've noticed that too. Things seem to be
improving all round.

PADDI   How do you feel about having more happiness
at work now? Is it important to you that we
do have more happiness?

MICH   Of course.

PADDI   Yes, but why is it important to you to have
         more happiness?

MICH   (*After some thought*) Well, it's important for
         me to have happiness at work so I can get a
         high score on the happiness meter!

I thought that Michelle felt that doing her job well (i.e.
performing as I wanted her to) was more important
than her personal happiness. It took me a little while to
realise she had her tongue firmly in her cheek.

What Michelle was really saying was:

> *When working towards a goal, it's very easy to spend
> so much time thinking about the score and looking at
> the scoreboard (for Michelle, the score on the
> happiness meter) that you miss enjoying the time that
> you spend working towards the goal.*

It is important to enjoy the 'journeys of life' because
the destination is not always what we imagined it
would be, and sometimes we don't even get there. Why
miss the view along the way!

 WHEN WORKING TOWARDS A GOAL, IT'S VERY
EASY TO SPEND SO MUCH TIME THINKING
ABOUT THE SCORE AND LOOKING AT THE
SCOREBOARD, THAT YOU MISS ENJOYING THE
TIME THAT YOU SPEND WORKING TOWARDS
THE GOAL.

INAPPROPRIATE GOALS

Sometimes, goals that we make for ourselves turn out
to be inappropriate. We reach them after an unhappy
struggle only to find that we have not really achieved

what we actually wanted, or the pleasure we receive from the achievement is not nearly as great as we anticipated.

Like a lot of people I have set goals that turned out to be inappropriate. I used to labour almost to the point of my own destruction so that I could have money to spend buying a little 'happiness'.

It took a lot of unhappy time to get me to the point where I could say that I was happy.

Buying Happiness with Unhappiness Can Be Inefficient

In general, people spend about eight hours of each weekday at work and much of the time they don't enjoy themselves. Like myself, people put up with this situation so that they can earn some money. In the small amount of leisure and holiday time that they have they take the money to buy things to try to make themselves happy.

It seems to me this process is inefficient in terms of the amount of pleasure received for pain. One sacrifices the greater part of one's waking time (the unhappy time at work), to be able to buy a little happiness in the leisure time. Not only that, but the time sacrificed is the daylight time when people are most awake, most alive and have the greatest capacity for enjoyment.

The things bought with hard-earned money then do not always provide the expected pleasure.

Whitsunday Washout

A few years ago I was anxiously anticipating a three-week holiday on the Whitsunday Islands; a tropical paradise in the north of Queensland. The trip would cost a lot of the money that I had earned during months of stress at work. I hung out for the time I would leave my unhappy workplace. The day I was to leave finally came.

Unfortunately, during the first week of my holiday I was still so stressed from work that I did not enjoy myself very much. The middle week was fun … well, not bad. I lay in the sun and swam, drank cocktails and worked on my tan. But, in the back of my mind was a niggling worry about work: How much harder I would have to labour when I returned so that my bank balance would be as it was before my holiday. The last week was quite spoiled because the niggle in my mind turned to trepidation as I anticipated my return.

On my first day back at work I felt as if I had never really had a holiday at all. I'd had only one somewhat happy week and it had taken me months of stressful work to pay for it!

If I had just aimed to be happy at work it would certainly have been a pleasant short cut compared to my holiday experience.

AIM TO BE HAPPY AT WORK INSTEAD OF GOING THE LONG WAY ROUND?

NO REBATES FOR TIME SPENT AT WORK

We have, they say, three score years and ten to live in this mortal sphere. After death perhaps we will stand before the Recording Angel.

The angel does not add up our time spent at work, treat it like injury time in a soccer match and say, pleasantly:

Oh, Paddi, I see that you have spent 64,000 hours at work. Of course we will give you a rebate for that. Here take this pink slip to the gatekeeper and he will see that you are credited this time and you can go back to earth again. See you in 64,000 hours. Be good!

This is my conclusion:

When we are at work we are living our lives.

I MAKE A CONFESSION

I have been taking you the long way around.

Deliberately, until now, I have not told you the answer that I gave to John's question. (You remember John the accountant?) I apologise, but I wanted to digress and make the point that happiness is more important than money.

Let's go back again.

JOHN E   Yes, I understand all you are saying about getting more happiness at work and I think its wonderful that you and your team have more pleasure in your work, but how can you make any money when you are spending all this time enjoying yourselves?

PADDI   When we spend our time enjoying ourselves we make more money!

Enjoying work increases profits!

Isn't the world a wonderful place! We can be happy at work and make more money precisely because we are

51

happy. This was a discovery I made gradually and it is only in retrospect that I understand the reasons behind it. Please let me explain what I discovered ....

WHERE'S THE PROFIT IN HAPPINESS?

Customers enjoy buying from businesses where the team members are happy. Happy team members tend to be more productive and have a long term commitment to their occupation.

WHERE'S THE PROFIT IN HAPPINESS?

---

*Customers enjoy buying from businesses
where the team members are happy.
Happy team members tend to be more
productive and have a long term commitment
to their occupation.*

---

ike everyone I have dealings with a number
of companies who are in the same generic
business, for example, hardware. I find that
the difference between the quality of the products in
the different businesses is very small. When I purchase
something, say a tin of paint, the quality of that
product as I the consumer judge it usually varies by no
more than ten per cent.

QUALITY AND PRICE

---

*Most people in business think that their customers
buy their product because it is better or cheaper. I
believe that whether or not a customer buys from
a business is most often determined by the people
in that business.*

With regard to price, I find that if I enjoy the company of the people who are selling an item to me, I am prepared to pay more than I would elsewhere.

I understand that some people are more price conscious than others. This may be because they have less disposable income, but perhaps it is because they have had less experience of good service. If service is perfunctory and impersonal, the price is the only variable. When people have experienced a pleasant relationship with a supplier they usually change that idea.

I often buy computer equipment. I could buy it in many places for rock bottom prices, but I don't. I pay 10–15 per cent more and buy from Nick and Malcolm who smile, are happy, friendly, helpful and polite. To me their warm smiles mean that they are happy in their work.

Unhappy business people don't have many smiles to share, they save them for their personal relationships and have too few left over for customers.

I like to do business with Nick and Malcolm because they smile at me.

I willingly pay a premium to deal with happy people and I am not the only one!

 WE ENJOY BUYING FROM HAPPY PEOPLE (AND WE DON'T ENJOY BUYING FROM UNHAPPY PEOPLE!)

Imagine that like me, a couple of years ago, you were looking for a leather bag to hold your Filofax, sunglasses, wallet, spare tissues and a pen.

Buying for Pleasure

People enjoy buying from happy people.

Illustrated by
Brian Doyle

Bag Shop

You are happy and the day is progressing pleasantly until you walk into a bag store and start to look around. There are a few bags that look interesting and one in particular, a little black number with gold clasp, catches your eye. It is within your preferred price range so you look around for the sales assistant. You locate her lurking in the corner behind the counter. She is unsmiling and her body posture tells you that at the very least she has just suffered a major loss on the stock market. She does not look happy. You smile at her and incline your head towards the bag in an unmistakable buying signal and thinking that a sale may improve her day.

She stares blankly at you, immersed in her own problems. Eventually she surfaces, sighs at the inevitability of having to provide service and ambles over. She is obviously sick in her spirit and as she approaches you can feel your own good cheer escaping. "Can I help you?" she manages. You indicate the bag. "I'm interested in that little black bag with the shiny gold clasp." With some effort she picks up the bag and disinterestedly hands it to you. She looks as though she would prefer to be somewhere else. You thank her and examine the bag. Making conversation in an attempt to cheer her you inquire about her day. "Terrible," she confides. "It's been a real busy week. Too many people in town. The boss is really pushing us and the senior salesgirl is a real bitch. Thank God it's Friday!"

Suddenly you feel surrounded by negativity and unhappiness. It is dragging you down and you want to escape. Mumbling an excuse you hand her back the bag, turn and run towards the door.

You locate the opposition bag shop. You meet a smiling sales assistant, who is cheerful and anxious to please. She sells you a bag and you leave her store clutching it, much happier than when you entered.

People don't enjoy buying from unhappy people — because it makes them unhappy too!

We like to spend our time with happy people — because their happiness spreads to us. We like to buy their goods and services so that we can please them and spend more time with them.

LONG HAUL TEAMS

There are many forces in the world around us that act to split our business team. People get sick, move, have children, change their skills, divorce, marry and die.

Team members who are happy in their work like to stay in their current team.

When major things happen in their lives that may tempt them to move house and job they think of reasons to stay where they are rather than leave.

When happy team members have minor sickness they work through their sickness — they would prefer to be at work with friends rather than moping at home.

I believe, and have some evidence to support this belief, that people who are happy in their work become sick less often.

With happy workers, if their spouse has the chance of a transfer, he or she is persuaded not to move. Those who improve their qualifications look for promotion in the same team rather than a new place to work.

Conversely, unhappy people look for reasons to move on.

When teams are split, those left in the team have to learn new relationships and teach skills again and again. This is time consuming, emotionally draining for all and a large hidden expense for the business.

THERE IS FAR MORE HIDDEN COST ASSOCIATED WITH HAVING TO TRAIN SOMEONE NEW, THAN WITH KEEPING A PRESENT TEAM MEMBER.

Some estimates put that hidden cost of locating and training at more than the yearly wage.

RELATIONSHIPS

Good team relationships have made us more careful of our language so that people's feelings are not hurt. Previously we weren't so careful with our words and, unfortunately, I was the worst offender

Relationships with your clients are heavily influenced by relationships within your team

A *Quick Recovery*

One day I was working in the surgery, with Pat, one of the Care Nurses. Pat passed the wrong instrument to me. I believed she had not been concentrating well enough and I said so. I said so in rather a sarcastic way. I felt a momentary pang of guilt for my actions, but I quickly assuaged it by resolving to apologise afterwards.

Lying on the dental chair below us, was a middle-aged business lady. I knew from my conversations with her that this lady had had a difficult time achieving the professional position that she currently held. She felt she had been unfairly discriminated against by some men in her organisation. She was not a misandrist ... but close to it. Certainly she was not chauvinistic for my cause of the moment — berating Pat.

Suddenly I saw my rudeness to Pat through her eyes. This Client had a friendly and trusting relationship with Pat; she knew me less well … and I had just been impolite and inconsiderate to someone that she liked and respected. A sudden saving grace gave me this insight into her thoughts about me. 'That Dr Lund must be an inconsiderate, uncaring, domineering male. He is not someone I want to do business with in the future!' This was not a beneficial image for me, when I was trying to build a trusting relationship with her.

I quickly apologised to Pat, immediately, and in front of the lady. Pat was happy for my consideration of her, and my relationship with the lady improved from that point. She seemed to trust me more than previously and she subsequently bought many of my services.

I learned two things from this incident and others that were to follow:

- There are humanistic reasons for politeness, but there is also the reason of good, old fashioned self-interest.

- Clients mirror our relationships.

When our clients see us, the working team, being unkind to each other they feel this is normal behaviour in our place of business and act in a similar way in their contact with us.

CUSTOMERS WHO SEE THE BUSINESS-FAMILY MEMBERS BEING KIND AND CONSIDERATE TOWARDS EACH OTHER SEE THEM AS PEOPLE TO BE TRUSTED. AND CUSTOMERS BUY MORE FROM THOSE THEY TRUST.

Why Not Fake it?

'Faking it' in regard to emotions, is prevalent in businesses.

It goes like this. The team members pretend to like each other and the customer, but it is such a chore, such an effort, that the charade is dropped as soon as the customer is out of earshot.

This leads to the following scenario:

Mrs Jones is complaining on the phone to the sales manager about the non-delivery of her order.

SM   (*Obsequiously*) I'm terribly sorry about your order Mrs Jones. I'll talk to Mr Malcolm, the salesman, about that. (*Aside to his secretary*). It's that #%@* Jones again. What a whiner!

By his words the sales manager has shaped his reality and also the reality of those around him. He has increased his antipathy to Mrs Jones and now his secretary probably doesn't think much of her either.

When the sales manager continues his conversation with Mrs Jones, no matter how charming he tries to be, some of his negative feelings towards her will leak out. If Mrs Jones is sensitive (and it's strange how sensitive customers are), she will detect these feelings. In the future Mrs Jones will probably not buy very much from his company.

CUSTOMERS BUY WHEN THEY FEEL THEY ARE LIKED — AND THEY CAN TELL THE REAL FROM THE FAKE.

ANGRY CUSTOMERS

A long time ago I remember reading an article about dealing with customers who are angry and complaining. The article advised saying nothing until angry customers have had their say. This, it explained, allows them to vent anger and they become calm.

At the time I was having problems of this type myself. People did complain and they did become angry and so I read the article with avid interest.

It is a number of years now since I had to face an angry customer. Of course we're only human and today things still do go wrong and customers do complain, but not in the same way. Now I find that customers voice their complaints in a more constructive way. They seem more empathetic and understanding of our failings and they point out the things they consider wrong or annoying without getting angry.

I think this change is because our customers realise that in our place of business it is not acceptable behaviour to become angry and abusive. Customers do not hear us raising our voices to, or being impolite with, each other and they respect the atmosphere that we have created. They are polite with us and this makes our life much more agreeable. Disputes are settled quickly and at less emotional cost. This is to everyone's advantage.

 CUSTOMERS WHO LIKE AND TRUST THE INDIVIDUALS IN A BUSINESS DON'T FEEL THE NEED TO GET ANGRY. THEY GIVE FEEDBACK THAT HELPS IMPROVE THE TEAM'S SERVICE AND INCREASE PROFITABILITY.

Feuds

When team members co-operate, the team is efficient. People who are unhappy find it hard to work together as a team and consequently the business makes less profit.

Unhappy people squabble easily and the disagreements are as commonly over small matters as large.

Squabbling makes the whole team less efficient as everyone tries to skirt around the problem and keep the protagonists apart. It is hard to be efficient when everyone feels like they are walking on eggshells.

Antagonism often seethes just below the surface and becomes a feud if the conflict remains unresolved.

I can remember silently feuding with Merilyn for a whole week.

Merilyn and the Feud

Merilyn and I didn't argue in public, but everyone knew to keep away from us and not to put us in a situation where we had to talk directly to one another. You could have cut the atmosphere with a knife. Everyone was upset. I spent most of the time being angry and demonstrating my anger. We managed to accomplish very little for the whole week. We were all on edge and too busy keeping out of each other's way to do much of a constructive nature. Everyone was caught up in the drama. Our customers of that week had a less than wonderful experience. I am sure that they noticed the icy atmosphere. Of course, we didn't make much money and I suspect the customers we saw were not keen to return for another unhappy experience ... and so our future income was also reduced.

I remember well the feelings I had that week, the anger and frustration, the tenseness in my chest and the feeling of powerlessness ... **but I can't for the life of me remember what our disagreement was about.**

I suspect that there are people who have been annoyed enough to kill someone and years later they think back and can't remember what they were fighting about.

As I look back over the disagreements I have had I find that they were almost never over large things, but almost always over the small things that seem too unimportant to worry about.

Most of us discuss the big problems in a calm and rational manner because we realise that they are too important to remain unresolved. It is the little things that, like pieces of shrapnel, slip under our shields. We don't discuss these small annoyances because they do seem so trivial, but when they are left unresolved, they fester and soon the relationship is painful and infected.

THE SEEMINGLY SMALL THINGS OFTEN CAUSE MORE INTERPERSONAL PROBLEMS THAN THE LARGE.

SABOTAGE AND NON CO-OPERATION

When team members have an unresolved difference at the very least they will not like working together, but they may also want to do a little more to make life more difficult for each other.

One member may sabotage another person's projects by practising passive resistance and non co-operation. Another may work more actively to reduce the success of a team mate's projects. Each may sabotage the work of the other in a tit-for-tat exercise and no matter how lowly one protagonist and powerful the other, there are still little ways to 'stick in the knife'.

When two people square off, they often attract a group of supporters who form cliques and take up the cause of one side or another. Soon the workplace resembles a battlefield with two or more factions who constantly bicker and snipe.

In some organisations sabotage by individuals or cliques goes on all the time and wastes much time and effort.

 FEUDS, SABOTAGE AND NON CO-OPERATION COST MONEY, BOTH DIRECTLY AND INDIRECTLY, IN THE PRESENT AND IN THE FUTURE.

It doesn't have to be like this.

Certainly it is not always easy for people in business to build caring relationships, but it is possible to make it easier — **by changing the environment and by creating systems that encourage closeness.**

POSITIVE
EMOTIONS
IN BUSINESS

Emotions in the work place have caused a lot of problems — but it doesn't have to be this way.

Positive Emotions in Business

Emotions in the work place have caused a lot of problems — but it doesn't have to be this way.

t the entrance to a business there is often a large invisible sign, emblazoned on which in large ghostly letters are the words:

Please park your emotions at the door before you enter.

Beneath, in smaller letters, are a few sentences by way of explanation.

If you want love or sympathy or joy or hope get it at home with your family or friends. We don't like employees to show emotion. It wastes time and distracts everyone from the real purpose of business: to make money.

Please note that the emotions that the sign refers to are the positive ones. It is a telling commentary on modern business that anger and distrust are often more acceptable than warmer feelings such as love, humility and kindness.

This sort of attitude is even enshrined in some workplace legislation proscribing friendly touching but not angry shouting.

Check Your Feelings

*Business Is War Inc. — Park your emotions at
the door before you enter.*

Illustrated by
Brian Doyle

HUMAN CONTACTS IN BUSINESS?

In this, the last decade of the twentieth century, most of us don't have the social contact in the way that people used to have within their extended families, churches, and community centres. Many of the institutions where we used to be able to share emotions and receive emotional support are going out of fashion.

People in today's society are often starved of positive human contact and, without these contacts, it is hard for us to be happy. Non-interactive pursuits like television, computer games, and spectator sports dominate many peoples' leisure time. This makes it very important that we have rewarding, positive social contacts at our place of work where we spend the greater part of our waking hours.

However, most businesses have so much experience of the negative type of feelings, such as anger, impatience and frustration, they are afraid to encourage more freedom for emotional expression.

Many business managers I talk with have difficulty even conceiving that it is possible for any business-family to work together in a modern productive business in peace, love and harmony. They have little possiblity of change. It is undeniably very difficult to achieve any outcome of which one can hardly conceive.

BUSINESS AS WAR!

There seems to be a general unconscious acceptance that negative emotions are normal and proper in business life.

More positive emotions, such as kindness and consideration, are sometimes seen to be a sign of weakness. We, in business, sometimes run our organisations as though we are an army fighting a war. There is no room for weakness — one has to be hard on the troops.

It is often accepted that:

- Anger can be expressed and used as a tool of oppression.

- Public ridicule is acceptable as a form of punishment.

- Coldness to subordinates maintains the hierarchical structure.

When those at the top of the organisation use emotional weapons for control of subordinates it comes as no surprise that the same weapons are used throughout the whole structure.

Similar aggressive methods are used to wage outright war against competitors and unions and there is a common opinion that to show kindness instead of this cut-throat aggression would be tantamount to business suicide.

EXPRESSION OF POSITIVE EMOTIONS AND VULNERABILITY

Most people involved in business have little difficulty identifying the negative, damaging emotions that permeate the majority of business workplaces. These emotions destroy relationships and also lead to a whole series of nasty games — games that are familiar to most of us in business: 'one-upmanship', 'bad-mouthing' and 'gossip' to name but a few. The stress, strain and time waste that are the inevitable consequences of these sorts of games are apparent to all.

However, most people who are in these businesses feel that there is no alternative to this system. It is little wonder when you stop to think how negative these people see their options, that stress in the modern workplace is so high.

The existing dynamics are painful, but the alternatives seem to involve the likelihood of even more pain.

The cessation of the destructive games seems only to be possible via the vulnerable ways of honesty, consideration, patience, love and honest communication, but in business, this approach is often seen as a weakness of which to take advantage.

It should come as no surprise that most people avoid vulnerability as they would some particularly nasty plague of lethal boils and warts. Those who try to be kind, happy and tolerant are open to attack on the aggressive business battlefield. They are often judged to be weak and may easily have their kindness thrown back in their face.

Having identified that human happiness (real business success) lay beyond the current business dynamics my business-family and I were left with little choice but to search for a safe way to use vulnerable elements in business so that we could get the benefits and avoid the pain.

With that in mind, we, at the PGL Dental Emporium, set out in our workplace to identify the sources of pain so that we could isolate and protect ourselves from them. We made a system of Performance Standards designed to prevent emotional burns and unfair judgements and so make it easier to open up — the Courtesy System.

I have found that when the Courtesy System is implemented in business it produces the change of attitude that allows freedom to express positive emotions without fear of retribution.

THE COURTESY SYSTEM MAKES IT POSSIBLE FOR PEOPLE ACTING IN A 'NICE' WAY TO SURVIVE AND PROSPER IN BUSINESS.

TO BE HAPPY WE NEED HAPPY PEOPLE ABOUT US

For the major part of humanity it is impossible to sustain happiness during prolonged isolation. Gaolers have known for centuries that a most distressing way to punish someone is to lock them away in solitary confinement.

We are social animals and we need our own kind around us.

Of course there are hermits who relish long periods alone, but I have never met one and I don't think they are a common breed. For me, a few hours by myself is pleasant and sometimes very desirable, but a longer period than this becomes disagreeable and I start to crave human companionship and interaction.

Evidence given in biographical reports about prisoners and kidnap victims shows that when they are kept in isolation captives will seek communication with anyone, even cruel gaolers in order to survive their solitude.

We need people! If you or I are isolated from other people for a long time I suspect that we would prefer anyone's company to none at all. One price we pay for our dependence on companionship is that *we are heavily influenced by those with whom we spend our time.*

Imagine that five of the most unhappy and negative people that you know are all gathered together in one room and you have to spend an afternoon with them. How happy would you feel at the end of the afternoon?

Similarly, if you had to work each day with morose, moody, uncooperative and discourteous people, I am sure that you would leave work feeling drained and cheerless.

The days that I remember spending with happy, positive people were invariably better than those with people who seemed unhappy.

This leads me to *Lund's Theory of Happiness: Part 1*

Lund's Theory of Happiness Part 1:
Spend more time with happy people and you will have more happiness.

HOW TO MAKE HAPPY PEOPLE

Do unto others as you would be done by.
Be kind to your neighbour.

This is the type of behaviour that makes those around us happy.

Religious leaders have been telling this to us for a long time. It is often called the 'Golden Rule'. The reason most commonly given to us to persuade us to be kind to others relates to rewards in the 'after life'. I think that there are more immediate benefits for us when we obey the rule.

Lund's Theory of Happiness Part 2:
You will become surrounded with happy people when you are kind, generous and loving to those around you.

Why am I telling you all this? Because I want you to be happy so that those around you will be happier, then those around them, and so on, until the effect reaches me. Selfish really, but I hope you agree, it could still be very effective and beneficial to all concerned.

SYSTEMS MAKE IT SIMPLE

Our environment influences our behaviour.

SYSTEMS MAKE IT SIMPLE

Our environment influences our behaviour.

ll of us may be affected far more than we realise by the environment in which we find ourselves. Efforts to improve our work environment pay handsome dividends both in our happiness and income.

In this context I use the term 'environment' quite broadly to denote the physical, social and political influences inherent in the situations in which one might find oneself.

I like to browse in bookshops, especially second-hand bookshops. Most especially I choose those that specialise in esoterica.

A Shocking Story

I was lurking around the stacks in one such shop when I came across a hard-covered book called 'Obedience to Authority', an unusual tome, written by the researcher, Stanley Milgram. It was written in the USA in the early sixties and at first glance was like one of the 'flying-saucer' books of the time: strange primitive-dialled machines, subjects strapped down, electric shocks … in a word: *weird*.

After I had read it for a while, I found it was really a well written and, to me, a scientifically sound book … it just seemed a little bizarre because the subject matter was unusual. The author described a series of experiments that had taken place in the US in 1955. The aim of the experiments ostensibly was to test the effects of punishment on learning. In reality, their purpose was to see how obedient people were toward authority.

The experimenters set up offices in the downtown area of a city. They advertised for volunteers who attended the office in couples and were met by a man in a white coat. The man explained the purpose of the experiment to them. (To test the effects of punishment on learning.) One of the volunteers became the 'teacher', the other the 'pupil'.

The teacher was given control of an apparatus that administered electric shocks to the pupil. This machine had a large control panel that varied the severity of the electric shock that the pupil received. The control was calibrated in volts and at intervals were placed descriptions of the effect of such a voltage on the average recipient. The descriptions ranged from 'Mild Shock', through 'Severe Shock' and all the way to 'Fatal Shock'.The pupil was placed in a room adjoining that of the teacher, out of the teacher's sight. The two could, however, hear each other. The teacher's part was to ask a question repeatedly and shock the pupil with increasing voltages until he answered the question correctly. (I told you this was *weird!*)

The experiment commenced. The teacher asked the questions and the pupil answered. If the pupil answered wrongly he was given a shock. As the questioning progressed and the voltage became higher and more painful, the teacher could hear the pupils' moans and screams from the adjoining room — chilling.

The man in the white coat was allowed only four things to say to the teachers when they became reluctant to continue (sic). These encouragements ranged from phrases like: 'You should continue' to 'You must continue or the experiment will be ruined'. Interestingly over 50 per cent of teachers would administer what were obviously fatal shocks.

Staggered at these results the experimenters moved the pupils so that the teacher could see the suffering they were causing. A large percentage of teachers still administered fatal shocks. **Some were even persuaded to hold the struggling pupil's hand down onto a metal plate to receive the shocks.**

What the teachers did not realise — until after the experiment — was they had not actually 'shocked' their pupils and that the pupils were professional actors trained to react on cue as if receiving a shock.

When the results of the experiment were first published it was not obvious in which country the experiment had been performed. The Americans surmised that it had taken place in a totalitarian regime, that people wouldn't act like that in a 'civilised' country. They were wrong!

The results of the experiment have been analysed and studied over the years.

The 'teachers' who gave 'severe' and 'fatal' shocks, did not seem to fall into a particular age group. There was no difference with regard to sex. Different socio-economic groups acted similarly. It seems that the situation in which people find themselves is, in some circumstances, a more powerful determinant of behaviour than is character or morality.

Similar experiments have been performed in more recent times and in a number of different cities with similar results.

One person who stands out in my memory of the Milgram experiment, was a lady who had spent some time in a concentration camp. She would not administer any shocks at all. She said she had seen too much suffering already in her life and she didn't want to see any more. To be forewarned is to be forearmed!

For me the story of this experiment has three useful lessons which are applicable to business.

- The environment in which we find ourselves may affect all of us far more than we realise.

- If we understand the profound effect our environment has upon us we have more chance to counteract it. (The lady from the concentration camp was in a position to understand how insensitive we can become to the suffering of others and how easy it is to abrogate our responsibility to 'Higher Authority'.)

- A change in our work environment can change our day-to-day behaviour.

Environment Can Enable Us to Act More Kindly to Each Other

If we find ourselves in an unpleasant environment our baser tendencies seem to rise readily to the surface.

A capacity for vindictiveness is within all of us. We do, after all, carry the genes of those of our ancestors who had to fight, hunt and kill, just to survive. Those forbears committed torture, rape, pillage and genocide — sometimes merely for pleasure. We are stuck with our genetic legacy but, if we understand ourselves well, we can compensate for those characteristics in ourselves that we find undesirable. A most effective way to do this is for us to carefully select and modify our environment.

If we find ourselves in an unpleasant environment our baser tendencies seem to rise to the surface. When we are in a pleasant, loving and supportive surrounding, we tend to sublimate these base characteristics and act kindly to our fellows.

People can be weak, violent, merciless, fickle, cowardly and inconstant. However, the selfsame people can, at other times, be noble, loving, generous and constant. Interestingly, when we are virtuous almost all of us are happier than when we are not.

The environment in which we find ourselves certainly influences our behaviour. The most powerful influence for me, and I think most other people, is the relationship and communication which we have with the people around us. We already have systems in our civilisations that regulate the way people deal with each other — social laws, common courtesy.

I think it is possible to make additional systems that complement and modify those that we currently use.

However, change is not easy to implement. I found the most important part of implementing any new system is **to build in the rewards that make it easier to continue with the system than to go back to the old ways.**

Making Systems Work — We Learn 'Customer-Speak'

A new system will work only when it is easier to use the system than to ignore it!

In one of our customer feedback sessions it was pointed out that it was bad enough having a mouth full of stainless steel instruments without hearing me ask for another 'carver' or an 'excavator'. We hadn't thought of these names as unpleasant because we were so used to them. To the person lying helpless and fearful, the words assumed much greater and more unpleasant significance.

The Doctor

I saw a film called 'The Doctor' a few years ago. It really made me think.

If you've ever seen this movie then you may remember the effect on the main character, a doctor, of his change in role from 'surgeon' to 'cancer patient'. The Doctor suddenly saw things from his patient's viewpoint. Things that to him, the surgeon, had been mundane became frightening to him as a patient. A receptionist who had previously seemed to him to be more caring than most, appeared to him, when a patient, as ruthless and cold. Even the x-ray machine seemed malevolent when he was in front of it rather than behind. The Doctor learned from his experience and when he recovered he went about his work in a more humane and caring manner.

As a team, a few years ago, we discussed the subject of the words we use.

We decided it would be a good idea to change our vocabulary. We brainstormed to think of less threatening words: to develop a new 'Customer-Speak' language.

- *Carver* became *Plastic*. (It was used for moulding plastic.)

- *Excavator* became *Spoon*. (It was shaped like a spoon.)

- *Probe* became *Michelle*. (A probe is for poking teeth and Michelle plays practical jokes on us all and pokes people behind their knees when they are least expecting it!)

But the change did not come easily. We all tried 'Customer-Speak' but we didn't succeed for very long. Pretty soon we had lapsed back into our old habits and words such as 'Plugger' still echoed around the surgery — and I was the worst offender!

We needed a system to facilitate and expedite effective change. We needed a system to make the change automatic. If we had a system that made it less painful to do the new actions than the old we could change more easily.

After we recognised that it wasn't easy I delegated the job of 'vocabulary policeman' to Joanne.

Joanne had only just joined the team and she knew the new 'Customer-Speak' words much better than she knew the old 'Jargon-Speak' words. Her job was to say the new word whenever someone (usually me) used the old. It is unpleasant being continually corrected, so we all changed rapidly and the new 'Customer-Speak' vocabulary became established.

There are many businesses that are still using 'Jargon-Speak' to communicate with their customers, not realising the communication barriers that they build.

SYSTEMS SET US FREE

Systems make difficult things easier.

During the hurly-burly of the average working day it is hard to keep one's own mind fixed on anything but the task in hand, that is, of course, unless the task has become automatic.

The more of our tasks we can make automatic, the more free we are to think about other things — new, more interesting and pleasurable things. We have more time to think creatively and to consider ways to improve our lives and businesses.

Systems take difficult operations and make them easier. Systems make complex tasks possible with little or no conscious thought, leaving us free to think and plan. Systems make it possible for us to free our brains while we perform habitual tasks.

If we do not evolve systems that make it possible for us to do relatively complex things automatically we waste a lot of our efforts thinking on the mundane.

The first time I made a photocopy on our new machine it took total mental focus. After I had read the instructions (the system) and practised a few times it became easy. Now I can make a photocopy while thinking of more complex problems.

 THERE IS AN INVESTMENT IN EFFORT TO DEVELOP IMPROVED SYSTEMS AND TO LEARN AND IMPLEMENT THEM, BUT IF WE DO INVEST THE EFFORT, WE GAIN MORE FREEDOM AND TIME IN OUR FUTURE.

'HI-TECH' AND 'HI-TOUCH'

Machines can take over the mundane tasks so humans are freed to do the things that only they can do: provide creative thought during the non-routine situations and bring the warmth of human contact.

When this works well it's called a 'Hi-Tech Hi-Touch' business.

Systems can also, like machines, provide the same freedom to their owners. If we systematise the regular, mundane work, then we are freed to concentrate on the more difficult times when we have to deal with people who are upset, fearful or unhappy and who require a warm, thinking, human touch. We can concentrate on these tasks knowing that the routine things are being taken care of by the system.

IF WE HAVE 'HI TECH' SYSTEMS TO COVER THE MUNDANE, WE HUMANS ARE FREED TO PROVIDE THE 'HI-TOUCH' TO THE MORE DIFFICULT SITUATIONS.

Mike Basch, one of the founders of the innovative American transport company, Federal Express, puts it another way,

Systematise the routine, humanise the exception.

OUR ENVIRONMENT CHANGED

In our dental practice we had already spent a lot of time systematising the clinical procedures: the way the instruments were passed, the order in which materials were mixed. We had done it to save ourselves time and effort.

Now for the first time we started to systematise our social behaviour. The dividends were rapid and obvious.

THE
COURTESY
SYSTEM

Revisiting the simple basics of Politeness.

THE
COURTESY
SYSTEM

Revisiting the simple basics of Politeness.

 hat is happiness?

I have certainly spent a lot of time thinking about this question and it's one that a lot of people have asked of me because they assumed that I was some sort of expert on the subject of happiness.

After all my cogitation I still don't know the total answer, but I am a lot closer than when I started.

I do know that happiness gives me a nice feeling. It's a feeling that makes me feel good inside, relaxed, at one with mankind and the universe. It's a feeling that I enjoy very much. For me happiness is not quite the same as 'fun' which is lighter and more mindless. Happiness is quieter and a little more considered. It's the opposite of sadness and better than contentment, which lies somewhere in the middle, but closer to happiness than sadness.

I have also learned something about how my happiness is achieved. For instance I feel happy relaxing on a warm beach with the sun shining and a small breeze blowing — but not for long. Sitting on a beach is fine for a while, but after a day or so I get restless and need some sort of constructive pastime.

The best kind of day for me is one where I do have a little leisure, but most of my time is spent pursuing aims that I find worthy or useful. The more of my goals or aims I reach in the day, the more I feel that my existence has some purpose and the more I feel some purpose in my life the happier I become.

I find I need to have systems and discipline in my life so that I do achieve something. The methods of achieving this discipline and systematising one's life and business are well documented in a plethora of business books. Even as a dentist, with no training at all in management, I had no trouble in finding books about systems to help myself and my business-family set goals and be productive.

No day however, can be a truly happy one for me and the rest of the business-family without pleasant social contacts. We need to give and receive the positive strokes that almost all human beings crave. Books that gave us systems to get positive strokes and avoid negative ones, were thin on the ground, so, as I have already indicated, we gradually developed our own system — the Courtesy System.

The implementation of this Courtesy System resulted in changes in the social and interpersonal part of our environment. When people were polite to us we felt warmth towards them and increasingly good about ourselves. Warmer relationships made even the building seem less cold and anyone who came in, clients, friends, suppliers, responded to the change in a very positive way.

The Courtesy System worked very well for us and led us down the path to centring our business upon Happiness.

POLITENESS IS THE OIL OF THE WHEELS OF SOCIETY

When I first started in private practice I had several admonitions on the wall of the waiting room. The one that sticks in my mind went something like this:

> Politeness is the oil of the wheels of society. It is even more important between married people than strangers.

I don't know who wrote it and I certainly didn't take much heed of it for the next 15 years, but eventually it started to make sense.

Most people believe that they should be polite to strangers. They know that if they are not, the strangers will not like them and not be polite in return. When strangers are not polite people feel offended and unloved: feelings that make for unhappiness and no one wants to be unhappy.

If it is important to be polite to strangers so that the social interaction we have with them makes for happiness, then surely it must be even more important to be polite to people who are intimates and have much more power to make our life unhappy.

The human race is an aggressive race and politeness and courtesy systems have evolved over long periods to make it possible to live close to one another in a society. Politeness is like diplomacy on a smaller scale and, like diplomacy, it keeps people from destroying each other.

THE COURTESY SYSTEM:
Performance Standard 1
Speak very politely using a person's name — 'please' and 'thank you' as a minimum.

HOW WE DO IT

DR L   Pat, I wonder if you would mind passing me the spoon, please?

PAT   Certainly Dr L. (*Pat passes the spoon.*)

DR L   Thank you Pat.

PAT   My pleasure.

Note the use of the softener 'I wonder if you would mind'. A softener reduces a command to a request. I could just as well have used, 'Would you mind' or, 'Could you just'.

Note also, 'My pleasure'. Pat may also have used, 'You're welcome', but some Australians object to that as being too 'American'.

IT'S NOT NATURAL!

When I tell people about this type of conversation they think it's really over the top for a dental surgery environment. They also think it is incredibly artificial and stilted.

Well, so it is, at first. Pretty soon it becomes automatic, part of normal social interaction and quite comfortable.

All social graces are learned. If our parents did not educate us in the niceties of social eating, everyone would feel nauseated when at the table in our company.

Social behaviour is something we are taught. It is not instinctive. We learn how to walk gracefully, not to eject gas from our bodies noisily in company and to blow our noses without contaminating those around us. Almost every behaviour we have has been learned and practised. Why not a few more?

When we first started acting so politely in the surgery we felt awkward. We thought that people would laugh at us for being so formal.

In fact just the opposite is the case. The most common comment of customers is:

> *Isn't it nice that everyone is so pleasant to each other around here. I wish it were like that at my work (or house)!*

Politeness affirms the dignity of the people with whom we communicate. When politeness is absent or too little is used, people feel slighted. When we stop to analyse why the cause of many heated disagreements cannot be recalled, it becomes obvious that it is not the topic of conversation that is most important as the fuel for emotional battles but the tone and words. It is the style of communication rather than the subject matter that most often give the perception that one's dignity has been affronted — that one is undervalued as a person.

Performance Standard 1 aims squarely at providing the continual affirmation of the importance of people to their peers. When team members feel safe and valued as people they can redirect the energy that would otherwise be used in protecting their self-esteem towards more constructive business efforts.

If I had been using Performance Standard 1 a few years ago when I had my disagreement with Merilyn, (see The Power of Courtesy) we would have both saved a number of days of pain, inaction and reduced income.

Here is a little story that may show you that not for everyone is this first Performance Standard as easy as it may seem.

Thank You Jack

Some time ago I was teaching the rudiments of the Courtesy System to a seminar class. I had just spent ten minutes describing the first Performance Standard. Before we moved on to the more difficult Standards, I wanted to show the group how simple it was to follow this one, to me the easiest of the Standards. The group was made up of intelligent people, for whom, I assumed, using this first Standard would be almost too easy. I divided the class into pairs and asked them all to role play in turn 'asking for a pen'. The appellant was required to say 'please' and 'thank you' as per the Performance Standard.

Each person played the scene in turn. The first four pairs had no problem, but one member of the fifth pair took two tries before getting it right. The sixth and seventh pair had no difficulty, but one of the eighth pair could not seem to say all the required words. I was a little nonplussed. I had thought there would be murmuring about the task being 'simplistic', instead one pair were having problems.

In this pair, the person having difficulties was a man who held an upper management position in quite a large business. He (I'll call him Jack) and I had had several conversations during the course of the seminar and I had found him to be well-spoken, friendly and intelligent.

The first time that Jack had asked his partner for the pen he had said 'Would you pass me the pen, thanks' I thought he was playing with me so I laughed good humouredly and asked him to try again — this time following the Performance Standard exactly. He look puzzled, and somewhat embarrassed. He tried again. 'I wonder if you would mind passing me the pen — thanks.' He looked pleased with his efforts so I passed onto the next pair.

Afterwards I talked with Jack. I was intensely interested in his difficulty saying 'please'. As I discussed the matter with him it slowly dawned on me that he honestly thought that he had said 'please'. He became a little annoyed at my probing, and not wanting to jeopardise our friendship, I let the subject lie.

Later I considered the matter and came to some conclusions: I surmised that Jack, being in a position of power in his business, was used to getting his own way. When he asked for something he inevitably received it. Perhaps to him that meant he could 'thank' the donor before he received, making it unnecessary to say 'please'. He was so much in the habit of using this construction that even when he believed he was saying something quite different he continued speaking in the same way.

This incident made me realise that using the Courtesy System was not so easy as I had imagined. Habits become ingrained, and we all have to try very hard if we want to change something so deeply implanted as everyday courtesy.

It is very easy to fall into the trap of disparaging people who are not around to defend themselves. Use this Performance Standard and it will become difficult to fall into this trap. Using peoples' names whenever we refer to them constantly reminds us to think of each one as a person. It leads us to find positive solutions to problems which involve us and them.

THE COURTESY SYSTEM

Performance Standard 2

When you talk about a person who is not present, speak as if they are listening to your conversation.
Use the person's name in each sentence in which you refer to them.

HOW WE USED TO DO IT

MERILYN That Fred Jones rang and cancelled his appointment at 10 am. It was for three hours!

PADDI (*Expletive deleted*) We should bill him for the lost time. Send him an account for three hours of our time.

MERILYN Okay.

HOW WE DO IT NOW (MOST OF THE TIME!)

MERILYN Fred Jones rang and cancelled his appointment at 10 am. It was for three hours.

PADDI That's inconvenient. Has Fred got a problem with that time?

MERILYN Fred said he had an urgent job to finish and he just wouldn't be able to get here. I don't think Fred realised that the appointment was so long.

PADDI Probably we should have explained to Fred more carefully how much time we had set aside for him.

MERILYN Perhaps we should both emphasise the length of the visit to Fred when we see him next time.

I am not saying that it is easy to change to this style of conversation. It was certainly not simple for us and we still have to take great care that we don't lapse back into our old ways, but benefits in improved relationships that have accrued have helped keep us on the 'straight and narrow'.

HUMANISING CONVERSATION

Using a persons' name in each sentence is initially awkward, but it is very effective in reminding us that we are talking about a real human being — someone like us.

The use of 'he', 'she' or 'them' makes it is easy to forget that 'he' or 'she' has feelings just like us.

When we talk about people who are not present and we are not very careful we could have a tendency to speak of them in a derogatory way and the conversation could slip towards gossip.

Gossipy conversations reinforce in the mind of the speaker and the listener bad feelings about the absent person. This reduces our chance of having a happy relationship with that person and, if they happen to be a customer or co-worker, the result may be a loss of income.

There used to be a feeling among our team that people who did not return for treatment did not appreciate us, or the service that we provided.

Jim of the Islands

I remember hearing from one team member about a man (Jim) who had not been to see us for a number of years and who, in pain, had phoned requesting treatment.

The team member said something to the effect that it was several years since Jim had been back for treatment and so obviously he was the sort of person who didn't care about his own health. Probably he would only want emergency treatment and not want to bother with saving the rest of his teeth. As I listened I felt myself become negative about the prospect of seeing someone who didn't care about himself or us. I concurred with the assessment of his character and spent a few moments complaining about people who didn't look after their dental health. All that day I was unhappy, not looking forward to treating Jim.

When Jim finally arrived I greeted him half-heartedly. Then we spoke a little. Jim explained that he had been working on one of the Pacific Islands for three years. He had returned the previous day. During his time away he had had no opportunity to return to us for treatment. Jim was desperately keen to save the tooth that he had damaged. In spite of our initial shabby treatment of him he subsequently became someone we looked forward to seeing. He was personable and kind to us. Jim had all his treatment and referred his friends to us for care.

There have certainly been times when I have fallen into the trap of talking people down and not been so lucky with the outcome as I was with Jim.

THE MEDICAL MODEL: PROBLEM FOCUS

There is a tendency in Medicine and Dentistry to refer to people by their condition and not by their names:

- The toothache at 5 pm.
- The gall bladder in room 302.
- The new ulcer next to that cardiac arrest.

The focus is placed onto the problem not the person.

It is an easy trap to fall into in our business and maybe in yours too; perhaps 'the tax problem guy' or 'that blond with the bunions'.

When we do refer to people by other than their names we dehumanise them and reduce the chances of having warm trusting relationships with them. Trust is vital in business and it is more easily achieved when people can relate to each other.

PERSONALISATION

What is in a name? A name indicates individuality. Each person can be grouped in some category or another, such as male, female, Caucasian, Italian or whatever — but a name gives us an identity of our own.

I remember reading an article investigating people who interrogate for a living. (Interrogate in this instance implies there was some physical as well as verbal persuasion during the process.)

The purpose of the investigation was to see what were the common traits in interrogators, that enabled them to torture others in their job. However, no difference was found to set them apart from 'normal' members of society. In fact, most appeared better citizens than the average. They were kind to their families, paid their taxes and donated to charities.

What was interesting was the way they talked about their victims. They did not refer to them by name, but by a derogatory epithet such as 'Subhuman', 'Slopey' or

'Chink'. They thought of their victims as less than human and therefore could more easily treat them as less than human.

They used a demeaning group name for the interrogatees, rather than their personal names, and this helped in the process of depersonalisation. It is easier to torture a 'Chink' than it is to torture Emily Wei, pharmacist, wife and mother, aged 29.

WAR

The military actually relies on this process of using words to dehumanise people and reduce the emotional content of inhuman acts to facilitate the otherwise repugnant task of killing and maiming fellow human beings.

In wartime, fraternising with the enemy is strictly forbidden and punished. Those in command try to paint the enemy as being inhuman, so it is easier for the soldiers to violate their normal moral repugnance for killing. The opposing army is spoken of in general derogatory and dehumanising terms, the nicest of which is the enemy.

Consider what would happen if, at the briefing before attack, the soldiers were told the following:

MAJOR   According to our intelligence you will be going up against the third regiment. Among the men involved are Peter Saab who will be driving the leading tank. It's his birthday today. His co-driver is Eric Cood. Intelligence leads us to believe that his wife has just had a baby — a little girl I think.

Once we think of people as human and we have some empathy for them it is more difficult to be nasty to them.

USING THE PERSONAL NAMES OF THOSE NOT PRESENT FOSTERS CARE AND CONSIDERATION FOR THEM.

DISCLOSING ONE'S NAME

At one time we didn't think it important that the nurses introduced themselves straight away. A nurse would walk into the waiting room and greet the client by name but not disclose her own name.

It is generally accepted in business and especially in the medical world, that the names of the clients are to be disclosed, but the personnel do not have to say their own names, they are there on their badges. (Can't people read?)

When I have been greeted, by name, by someone who has not introduced themselves to me, I find it irritating and when I am in a situation where I am not feeling confident, I find it degrading!

THE COURTESY SYSTEM

Performance Standard 3

If you have a problem with someone, talk about the problem only with them, and in private.

ONLY WITH THEM

In my experience communicating with some one other than the person with whom you are having the difficulty rarely solves a problem.

If anything the problem become worse. The person with whom you discussed the problem often tells another person. They tell another and another. The story becomes distorted in the telling and retelling.

It is amazing how a message or the description of an incident can become distorted by passing through a series of ears, brains and mouths. Especially this is so when we introduce the normal human propensity to exaggerate to make a story 'juicy'.

Eventually the now greatly modified version of events gets back to the person with whom you were having the problem.

They are annoyed to think you have not talked it over before telling the 'whole office' and they become even more upset when they discover the 'wicked lies' you have told about the incident.

IN PRIVATE

In the past I found the guidance that I gave was not as effective as I expected.

It took a little while but eventually I realised why this was so.

When I felt someone needed my help and advice I would give that help and advice as soon as I detected a problem. My reasoning was:

- When someone makes a mistake you must point out their mistake straight away or they won't learn to do better — 'strike while the iron is hot!'
- In my busy day it's hard for me to remember to give the guidance later.

Unfortunately for the one being advised when I gave the guidance, other people were usually around and listening. The listeners became an audience and it was the presence of that audience that caused what would otherwise have been seen as guidance to be perceived as a punishment.

It was hard for the recipient to hear and accept my advice while feeling embarrassed at being in front of an audience.

I gave the guidance in what I felt was a firm, but fair manner. I walked away and forgot all about it, but the recipient was left feeling small, hurt and resentful. This resentment that my advice produced meant that, even if I had given good advice, it was likely to be ignored. Worse still the level of trust in the relationship was frequently impaired.

 EVEN THE MOST KINDLY, WELL-MEANT AND CONSTRUCTIVE CRITICISM TAKES ON A MUCH HARSHER TONE WHEN IT IS GIVEN IN PUBLIC AND OFTEN IT DOES NOT HAVE THE DESIRED RESULT.

THE COURTESY SYSTEM
Performance Standard 4
Apologise and make restitution if someone is upset by your actions.

It seems really hard for many people to apologise when they have made a mistake. Perhaps they feel that people will judge them weak. It may be that they think that if they don't apologise the mistake will be more quickly forgotten.

As I go about my life as a consumer, there have been many times when I felt I deserved an apology, but few times that I have received one. You may have had the same experience.

It has been my experience that, in business, far from causing us more problems, an apology gains us more goodwill from our customers and co-workers.

Undeveloped Relationship

I had a film to be developed so I took it to the local photo shop. (*Giant automatic processor. Ready in 60 minutes. Free film with your prints!*)

It was 11 am when I left the photos with a personable young man. I waited in the coffee shop and returned at 12 noon when they were due to be finished. The photos were not ready. The young man explained that he had been very busy serving other customers and that my photos would be ready in ten minutes. He was pleasant enough, but gave no apology. I returned ten minutes later and the photos were ready. He gave them to me and explained that, since I had had to wait ten minutes, the second set of photos were free but he still didn't apologise for keeping me waiting.

So I paid $14 instead of $18. Good deal? Well, yes, I was $4 better off, but I still didn't feel good inside. I felt he owed me an apology and I wasn't really happy. I almost felt cheapened by the gift of money — as if my goodwill could be purchased for $4. If he had just said 'I'm sorry I kept you waiting' I would have felt good (He really only kept me ten minutes) and he could have kept the extra $4 which was probably a major part of the profit.

I am sure the young man felt he was doing the right thing and indeed he did perform a lot better than the staff of the opposition photo shop, but he could have done so much more to make his customer (me) happy, with just a small apology.

When people apologise they are not seen as weak or stupid; on the contrary, because so few people are brave enough to admit an error and apologise gracefully, people who do are seen as courageous, strong and honest.

BRAVE (AND SMART) PEOPLE APOLOGISE.
WEAK (AND NOT SO SMART) PEOPLE DON'T.

THE LOST CAP

When people who have caps on their back teeth chew sticky lollies they can pull off the cap that we have placed. We warn people against chewing these foods, but some still do it and, as a consequence, displace their caps a day or two later when they have forgotten their sticky transgression.

Often clients feel that if they don't stand up for their rights they will be charged for having their cap re-cemented.

When customers believe that they have to fight for their rights they become aggressive and demanding.

In the past, when this happened and a customer came in with cap in hand, I became equally aggressive.

Scene 1: At the PGL Dental Emporium, circa 1985.

CUST   My cap has come out

PADDI   (*Accusingly*) What have you been eating?

This statement was designed to transfer the blame. It was not that I had fitted the cap badly, it was the user who had exceeded the specifications or not followed the instruction to avoid sticky foods!

CUST   (*Defensively*) It wasn't my fault. (*And then one of the following...*)

I was only chewing a tiny piece of bread.

It was only mashed potato.

I was only breathing and it just fell out.

PADDI   (*Critically and disbelievingly*) Hrmm!!

CUST   Can you put it back again?

PADDI   Well, yes I can, of course, but you do realise that I will have make a charge for that?

And so I put the cap back and, with bad grace, the customer paid.

I felt justified charging and not tendering an apology. It wasn't my fault that the cap came off. Why should I apologise?

If that client ever had to have another cap, you can bet he didn't come back to see me!

It reminds me of an epitaph on a gravestone that I learned as a child. I'll tell it as I remember it, but that may not be exactly as it was engraved.

This is the story of Jonathan Grey,

Who died maintaining his right of way.

105

His way was right and his will was strong,

But he's just as dead as if he'd been wrong

I stuck to my guns. I felt I was right, but I suffered for my inflexibility.

Luckily for me, (and the customer), as time has gone by I have learned to apologise.

Scene 2: At the PGL Dental Emporium; the present.

CUST   My cap has come out.

PADDI   I'm sorry that you are having that problem, I'll put it back for you straight away. Of course there will be no charge for that.

CUST   Thank you. (*I replace the cap.*)

PADDI   Once again I'm sorry that you had that problem. Of course you don't have to pay for having it put back. By the way, Kate has just baked some fresh Fruit Salad Dental Buns and we have made up a little basket of them. I hope you will accept them as our gift to you for your inconvenience.

CUST.   Thank you, but I really think I should pay, because I was eating a sticky lolly and you specifically warned me about that.

Interesting isn't it?

WHAT I HAVE LEARNED IN 10 YEARS

It doesn't matter who's fault it is, it is to everyone's advantage if I accept the responsibility and put things right.

The customer is the one who decides who has the blame.

If I can succeed in helping the customers to be happy about the incident, they will probably continue to give me their custom.

I have noticed that when I apologise, put things right again and make some restitution, people become better customers than they were previously.

THE COURTESY SYSTEM
Performance Standard 5
Greet and farewell everyone by name, with eye contact and a touch.

This Performance Standard is about deciding whether people or tasks have the greater importance.

HOW WE DO IT

I arrive at the office.

I walk around to all the places where the team members tend to congregate. I greet each in turn.

PADDI   Good morning Gloria, Morning Pat, Hi Michelle!

As I greet everyone, I look them in the eye and I touch them or they touch me. The way that we touch varies from person to person and day to day. Sometimes it's a kiss, sometimes a hug, sometimes a pat on the back or an American type 'High Five' — or whatever both people are comfortable with.

As each person arrives they do the same with those already at the office.

WHY DO IT?

Before this Performance Standard, the best that we could manage was to enter a room and say 'Hi!' or 'Bye!' Rarely would we use a name. Mostly we were too busy or rushed to do either.

Now, if someone says 'Hi!' to me, it's better than no greeting at all, but how much more pleasant it is if I hear 'Hi Paddi!' It gladdens my heart to hear my own name and I feel kindly towards the person who used it.

We all like to hear our own name and, when it is used in greeting or farewell, it increases the bond which joins us to the speaker.

We work to increase bonds within our team. The more we have invested in a relationship and the more we get from it, the less likely we are to do something that damages that relationship.

As I look back on my life in business I realise how often I played games to make me feel important. One of those games was 'I am too busy doing things to bother with you.'

When someone started to talk to me I would look up from what I was doing with an irritated, pained expression, as if to say:

I am working really hard here on very important things. These things are so urgent and consequential that you are being presumptuous to think that any communication I could have with you would even approach the importance of what I am doing.

I assumed that my inquirer would then be very impressed with my industriousness and status.

Now I realise what it really means when I am too busy to acknowledge someone. It means that I am stupid enough to have packed my life with so many 'things' that I don't have time for the most important thing in life — 'people'. People are most important to me because they affect my happiness more than 'things'.

It is important to make time for personal contacts and the most important time for this is at the beginning and end of the day.

At the beginning of the day when two people greet each other they set the tone for any further contacts they have throughout that day. At the end of the day the farewell fills their memory with kind thoughts of each other to take home and add to the credit in each others emotional bank account.

Don't Call Me 'Dad'!

My daughter Kate first started working with me before we had implemented Performance Standard 5 and before I understood the power of names.

Understandably, she was used to calling me 'Dad' and she continued to do so at the office. I took her to task because I thought it more seemly if she called me 'Dr Lund' in front of clients. I felt that it would dilute my image to have me called by such a familiar name when I was a professional person. Kate convinced me that I was being pompous, so with some trepidation, I became 'Dad' to her once more.

So far the reaction I have received has been overwhelmingly positive. Clients who hear me called 'Dad' see me as more human than previously. More importantly for me, every time I hear 'Dad' I sense a deepened bond with a daughter, I feel more a person, less a dentist and I work more humbly, sensitively and happily.

WITCH HUNT

What happens in your business when something goes wrong? If your business is like most, you begin what is called the 'Witch Hunt'.

The purpose of the 'Witch Hunt' is to find someone to blame and punish for causing the problem. Just as in the Witch Hunts of Salem, the best victim is the person who can least defend themself. The lower the status of the scapegoat, the less they are likely to complain or divert blame to others.

The purpose of the punishment (nowadays more verbal than thermal) is to help everyone (except the scapegoat) to feel better about themselves — to feel absolved of sin because any shared blame is taken on the shoulders of the witch. The ritual sacrifice appeases the gods of business — for a time at least.

THE COURTESY SYSTEM
Performance Standard 6
Blame a system not a person.

In my experience, almost always at the root of business problems is a defective or an inadequate system — not a person.

The problem with the 'Witch Hunt' is that it rarely solves the underlying problem and the same problem often recurs again and again requiring more sacrifices.

A fear begins to pervade the lower reaches of this sort of organisation as people wait for the axe to fall (or the faggots to burn!). People find excuses to do nothing for fear of doing something wrong and attracting blame.

'WITCH HUNTS' DO NOT USUALLY SOLVE THE UNDERLYING PROBLEM AND THE UNDISCLOSED FEAR OF PUNISHMENT LEADS TO ORGANISATIONAL PARALYSIS.

WITCH HUNTS OR DRAGON SLAYING?

The only real cure for 'witch burning behaviour' is to make good systems and remove the bad systems — kill the Wicked Systems Dragons.

If only we could be a business hero, take our courage in both hands and go out to slay the Wicked Systems Dragons, all could live peacefully. Instead we often take the easy, cowardly way out and, with the other townspeople, catch and burn any poor witch or warlock that happens to be in our power and the Systems Dragons continues on their periodic rampages.

IT'S FAR BETTER TO SLAY DRAGONS THAN TO BURN WITCHES.

Backup Blues

I was talking with Joanne a while ago, asking her about 'Witch Hunts' and if she had noticed any difference since we started blaming a system and not looking for a person to denounce. Joanne was the most junior person in our organisation so I surmised that she would have noticed the greatest change.

The Systems Dragon is Loose!

Witch Hunts do not usually resolve the underlying problem. Blame the System, not the person.

Illustrated by
Brian Doyle

Joanne was effusive in her praise of Performance Standard 6. "It's great", she said and then, a little poignantly, "Now I don't get blamed for anything." "What do you mean", I said, a little taken a back that things had obviously been so bad for her in the past.

"Well", she continued, "when things used to go 'wrong' and there was nobody obviously at fault, it was always me who got the talking to. It wasn't always said that it was my fault, but it was still me who was shown the problem and me who was looked at when someone said that this mistake shouldn't happen again. Often it wasn't anything to do with me and so, the same problem occurred again and again, because nobody knew who was really responsible, or what system we should be following, and I was too shy to say anything."

"For instance, take the computer backup. If the backup didn't go through correctly it was always me who was hauled over the coals, and sometimes I hadn't even been in the day that it was done."

"Now we have a system. We have to exit from all of the workstations before we start up the backup program, then we put in the correct tape and start it up. Whoever runs the program has to initial each box on the backup system sheet and write down the name of the tape used and the type of backup they are doing. In the morning, whoever starts up the computers has to verify that the backup is completed and also initial the box on the backup system sheet. It's simple!"

"Before this system there always seemed to be one workstation computer that was left running and so the backup didn't work properly. Everyone blamed everyone else (but mostly me). Now whoever initials the box is responsible and because someone is obviously responsible for each step it always gets done correctly and I don't get it in the neck any more. It's wonderful to have a system."

The backup system took some time to devise and some more time and effort to print the relevant sheets, but now it always runs correctly. My mind is at ease, Joanne feels happier and we don't waste time on 'Witch Hunts'. Systems are great! They stop people being unhappy!

WHY THINGS GO WRONG

In my experience almost always at the root of business problems is a defective or an inadequate system. W. Edwards Deming, the American statistician who taught Total Quality Management to post-war Japanese business, believed that 85 per cent of quality problems are caused by defective, inadequate or missing systems and only 15 per cent are caused by deficiencies in the people using the systems.

Very occasionally someone makes a deliberate mistake, but this is rare. Most people want to perform their jobs well. Few like to fail or be seen as inadequate.

MOST PEOPLE WANT TO BE 'GOOD'. IT IS BAD SYSTEMS THAT MAKE THEM 'BAD'.

THE COURTESY SYSTEM
Performance Standard 7

Tell the truth.

A few years ago we were in the habit of making up stories to cover our own inefficiencies. If something went wrong it was always the fault of the 'laboratory', or the 'suppliers'.

In spite of the fact that I had read and been taught since childhood about the virtues of truth, it was only after the following incident that I really believed this.

Truth, Glorious Truth

A client, Eric, arrived to have a cap fitted ... but it had not been delivered from the laboratory. By a little detective work, we found that we had given the laboratory the wrong date for the return of the finished cap and they would not have it ready until the next day. Eric was Merilyn's client so she had to provide him with an explanation. We were working together trying to think of a plausible story when I suggested it may be interesting to tell him **the truth**. (OK for me because I didn't have to do it.) Merilyn, very bravely I thought, said that she would give it a try.

We all waited in the wings, listening. Merilyn told Eric what had happened and how we had messed things up. She apologised and we all waited for the storm. Eric laughed! He laughed quite loudly and commiserated with Merelyn.

We were all agreeably surprised and indelibly impressed with the power of the truth.

I spoke earlier about Mrs Jones complaining on the phone to the sales manager about the non-delivery of her order. You may remember the conversation:

SM   (*Obsequiously*) I'm terribly sorry about your
        order Mrs Jones. I'll talk to Mr Malcolm, the
        salesman, about that. (*Aside to his secretary*)
        — It's that #*?@ Jones again, what a whiner.

The conversation continues:

SM	(*Charmingly*) Yes. I'm sure Mr Malcolm is competent, he is one of our most trusted and valued employees. It's probably a problem with the post.
MRS J	Thank you for your help. (*Rings off*)
SM	Send for that #&@% Malcolm. He's screwed up again. I'll have his hide. That's his last mistake for this company!

Next time Mrs Jones' order is dealt with by another salesman who gleefully tells her that Mr Malcolm has been fired for his part in her problem and that he (the new salesman) will be much more careful.

The truth has a way of coming out. Mrs Jones understands that the Sales Manager lied to her and the Sales Manager's secretary is caught up in this same deceit.

Mrs Jones will not be so keen to deal with this particular company again.

CUSTOMERS DON'T LIKE TO BUY FROM THOSE THEY SEE AS DISHONEST.

TRUTH KEEPS THINGS SIMPLE

Even when we feel we are expert in hiding the way we feel, we sometimes inadvertently reveal the true nature of our feelings by the little unintended, unnoticed verbal and non-verbal 'give-aways' that pepper our communications.

Tone of voice indicates whether or not someone is being sincere. We can sense warmth or interest and recognise insincerity from facial expressions and body posture.

People in general are no more stupid than you or I and, like us, are able to interpret the inflections in speech that give the lie to what is being spoken. A successful liar has to have a remarkable memory and, in the complexities of business, it is hard to keep track of the odd little untruths said on the spur of the moment. Unless each one is recorded and can be accessed readily, unwelcome complications can arise and cause much trouble and even expensive litigation.

TRUTH KEEPS THINGS SIMPLE AND IT'S CHEAPER IN THE END.

COURTESY SYSTEM
Performance Standard 8

Use positive conversation.

Avoid, fatalism and other dis-empowering speech. Murphy's Law is a good (bad!) example of this. You remember what Murphy said: 'Anything that can go wrong, will go wrong and at the worst possible moment.'

INTERESTING OPPORTUNITY

A friend once told me that there is a language that doesn't have a word that is an exact equivalent of our

English word 'Problem'. The nearest equivalent in that language is 'Interesting opportunity'. Now I don't know whether this is true or not and I haven't discovered which language it is, but it serves as a convenient illustration for the following point:

Should someone say to me that I have a problem I get a negative picture, I have the feeling that I could fail in overcoming this problem and, at best, there is going to be a struggle before I win.

However when someone says to me that I have an interesting opportunity coming up I have a positive feeling and almost a sense of excitement. I am going to do something new and I am going to succeed.

Imagine how differently we would approach difficulties if our language also did not contain the word 'problem'!

THE POWER OF WORDS

Language is very powerful. It is one of the tools we all use to shape our reality. We think in pictures, feelings and words. If we hear enough fatalistic statements we become fatalistic ourselves and this shapes our reality.

The type of language I hear and use determines my view of life. If I think of life as a raging torrent that carries me along wherever it wishes and can drown me or place me gently on dry ground, according to its whims, it is hard for me to take control of my life.

If, conversely, I find life to be like a calm river that meanders along and I am the boatman punting from shore to shore, faster or slower as the mood takes me, I am empowered and feel in control of my life.

How often have you heard something like the following:

Wouldn't you know, I was rushing to find a parking spot in the rain and just as I got there someone else pinched it. After about half an hour cruising around fuming, I finally spotted another and just as I stopped to get it an idiot bashed into the back of me. I bet before this day is finished something worse will happen. Bad luck always come in threes.

Of course another problem will arise. When people talk and think like this they invite one. Another example is:

We are so close to making this deal, but I just know something is going to spoil it. It's Murphy's Law. You can't win. Just when you think you finally made it Old Murphy pops his head up and whoops down you go, at the worst possible time, right at the touch line!

These attitudes are disempowering for everyone.

With negative language we can make each other fatalistic and powerless.

 BY HABITUALLY USING LANGUAGE THAT IS EMPOWERING AND FOCUSES ON OPPORTUNITIES, WE CAN CREATE A NEW MORE POSITIVE REALITY FOR OURSELVES AND THOSE AROUND US.

Performance Standard 8 is the latest of the performance standards that we have made and attempted to live by. It has proved to be quite difficult to implement. Our lives and conversations are so filled will the negative that it has been hard for us to change.

To help myself with this problem of negativity I have stopped listening to the news on the television and I avoid newspapers. A lot of the media is so filled with the bad things in life that they make it harder to feel that there is good in the world.

Some of the news media seems to have a prurient interest in murder and mayhem. Often what seems to threaten the neighbourhood is in fact occurring in a distant part of the country or even another part of the world. This makes people paranoid and suspicious of all those around.

I believe that the overwhelming majority of people are basically good, but if I spend a lot of time informing myself from the news media, I get the impression that most people are bad and that view comes to be reflected in my conversation and actions.

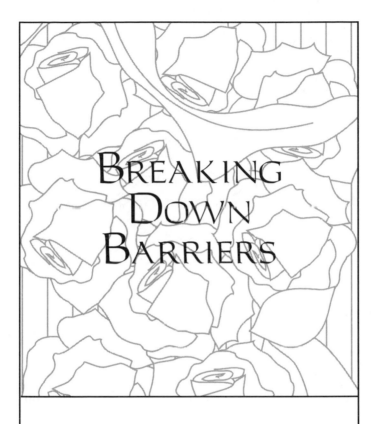

BREAKING DOWN BARRIERS

When your business-family members have become happier by using the Courtesy System they are in a better position to build warm relationships with their customers. This warm relationship will lead to more business.

BREAKING
DOWN
BARRIERS

When your business-family members have become happier by using the Courtesy System they are in a better position to build warm relationships with their customers. This warm relationship will lead to more business.

conventional business wisdom seems to encourage the creation and maintenance of barriers between people so close contact is avoided.

Nowhere do we see this more than in the 'traditional' professional office. For many years I had a traditional office.

When I started off in my own practice, like almost all professional people, I had a front desk, a waiting room and a receptionist. I used 'burning' and 'sawing' to change the system. Here are a few of my thoughts on and experiences with the barriers between team and customers.

Bridge Burning

The front desk sat, monolithic, directly in front of the entry. It marked the boundary between the territory of the team and the territory of the customers, giving us

Management by Chainsaw!

*The Dentist rids himself of a barrier and
'burns his bridges'.*

Illustrated by
Brian Doyle

a feeling of security, with something to keep the 'foe' at bay. The receptionist greeted the clients from behind the desk, made small talk and asked them to wait until we were ready to see them.

All conversations were carried out in front of the other occupants of the waiting room. The nurses escorted the clients into the surgery and stayed with them for the duration of their treatment. The client was then escorted back to the receptionist who made the next appointment for the client, again in front of the others in the room.

When we started to enjoy more warm contacts within our team it struck me that the reception desk was a great barrier to good communication, so I had three small lounges built for clients and team members to have some privacy for their conversations. Everyone in the team thought the lounges a wonderful idea, but nobody used them. It was too easy to continue in the old way with all transactions conducted at the front desk. I felt very frustrated and, one weekend, I decided to take radical and irreversible action. With a large motorised saw and the help of Merilyn's husband Barry, I sawed up the reception desk.

On Monday morning there was instant and widespread confusion. Like a crowd of perplexed, angry bees everyone milled around the place where the reception desk had stood. No one knew what to do when the first client of the day arrived, but soon a pattern was established. The client was greeted at the door and then taken to one of the small lounges — the result that we had all intended but had been unable to implement.

Julius Caesar and his army crossed over the River Rubicon on their way to battle. After his army had crossed over, so that there was no retreat for them, Caesar had his engineers burn the bridge. The army unable to swim in their heavy armour had little choice but to go forward — there was no way back without a bridge. And on they went — to victory.

We had been unable to produce the effect we wanted by just wanting it. Like Julius Caesar I had to burn the bridge so that there was no going back. So we proceeded — victorious.

(I must insert a caveat here. If the team is very unhappy about the change this sort of high handed behaviour can result in a lot of resentment with ensuing retribution. Remember, the Ides of March come annually.)

Bridge burning can force changes that previously seemed too difficult to implement.

The 'Care Nurse' System

We deepened client/nurse relationships by allotting each client their own, personal 'Care Nurse.'

It used to be that each of our patients took potluck as to who was to care for them during their visits to the surgery.

Because we wanted a deeper relationship between nurse and client, we changed the system so that a customer always saw the same nurse. By and by the relationship between Care Nurse and client did deepen. It became common for the client to receive calls after hours from their Care Nurse inquiring about their welfare after their treatment, confirming appointments, or congratulating them on important events in their life. The Care Nurses would gladly make calls even in their own time.

The things that marred the new relationship were problems with debts and accounts.

New Age Accounting

We used to have one person to send out accounts. She was very good at figures, quick at typing and not afraid to confront people about their debts, so she was the obvious choice. Our accounts-lady certainly handled the job very well. She always had the bills out on time and she always followed up with telephone calls if there was no response to the letters. She seemed very persuasive on the phone and she even arranged for our debtors to go to the small claims court when it was necessary. Our Accounts Receivable were around the industry average and we had about 5 per cent bad debts. When our accounts-lady had to leave, the Care Nurses took over the accounting. They did the billing and receipts for all of their own clients and we no longer had centralised accounting and billing.

There was an interesting spin-off — because the clients now had a lot more invested in the relationship with their Care Nurse they were more reluctant to jeopardise it by being tardy with their payments. Now that there were good communications any problems with accounts were quickly ironed out. Our bad debts and accounts receivable dropped amazingly!

The Care Nurses had no formal training in debt collection or accounting. To my mind they were successful in improving our accounts receivable and bad debts, not because they were better at asking for the money, but because they had a close relationship with their clients, something the accounts-lady did not have.

WARM RELATIONSHIPS ARE OFTEN MORE IMPORTANT THAN GOOD TECHNIQUE.

Warm relationships are not automatically a result of good service. Here is an experience of mine which I think illustrates this point.

High Class Restaurant

One Saturday night some time ago, my wife Debra and I went to the theatre to see a play. After the performance we decided to treat ourselves to a meal at an expensive Brisbane restaurant.

At the door of the restaurant we were greeted by a charming *maitre d'hotel* who introduced himself and showed us through opulent surroundings to an impeccably laid table. He passed us the menu, wished us *bon appetit* and left. Soon we were visited by a waiter who took our food order and then by a wine waiter who advised us about the wine choices. A few moments later a different waiter arrived to give us bread rolls, then still another delivered the chefs' complementary appetiser. A fifth presented us with our entrees and wine. Throughout the evening we were treated to a procession of efficient, smiling waiters. I noticed that everyone in the restaurant was having the same type of experience — a procession of waiters who would go from one table to another, rarely to return.

As the meal progressed we started to see a few familiar faces returning to our table. It was like watching a merry-go-round as faces appeared, disappeared and eventually returned. The food was wonderful, the surroundings were all that one could wish for and the waiters were unobtrusive, smiling and skilful, but neither Debra nor I enjoyed our evening. A potentially wonderful night was spoilt by a system that did not allow the waiters time to develop a relationship with us.

There were plenty of waiters to see that everyone had wonderful service. Each waiter who served us introduced himself with a smile, but there was no continuity of conversation with any single one of them. Each of them dutifully asked if we were enjoying our meal or wine. We answered, but with increasing annoyance, because we were answering the same question over and over — not the waiters' fault! Each one did his best to make us feel special, but ignorance of the questions asked by the others and of our answers made their task very difficult.

Whoever designed the service system did not understand that it is not always enough for customers to know a name, to see a smile and to have attentive service.

IT IS IMPORTANT TO IMPLEMENT A SYSTEM TO TRAIN FRONT LINE PEOPLE TO GIVE EXPERT SERVICE, BUT IT IS EVEN MORE IMPORTANT THAT THE SYSTEM ENCOURAGES AND ALLOWS WARMTH AND BONDING WITH CUSTOMERS

Debra and I have not returned to that restaurant; we have found other places. One of these is a less sumptuous restaurant where, compared with the place I have just described, the food was certainly inferior, the decor less opulent and the staff fewer.

Enrico — A Real Person

The first time we ate at this little place we were served by only one person throughout the meal — Enrico. Enrico was competent at his job, but not polished. However we achieved a level of communication that we found most pleasurable. We left at the end of the meal, very satisfied and promising ourselves to return soon. We did return, on a number of occasions, partly to fill our stomachs, but partly to see Enrico, our waiter. He was not consistently expert as he served us, or even always alert to our needs. He was not always in a good mood, but at least we knew him as a real person and he remembered us.

Customers need to believe they are cared for, even if only a little. Waiters need to believe they are cared for, if only a little. Each needs the other. Waiters who feel kind feelings from their customers enjoy their jobs and serve their customers warmly and attentively. Customers thus served show their appreciation in many small ways. This makes the waiter feel cared for too and they want the customer to visit again.

Both parties need the time and opportunity to build such a relationship.

CUSTOMERS RETURN TO PLACES WHERE THEY FEEL CARED FOR. WAITERS WHO FEEL APPRECIATED BY THEIR CUSTOMERS ARE LIKELY TO STAY FOR A LONG TIME IN THE SAME EMPLOYMENT.

THE SYSTEM IN ACTION

It is not easy to change the way the people in an organisation work together, but it can certainly be worth the trouble. The Courtesy System provides the framework for a better way of doing business.

THE SYSTEM IN ACTION

It is not easy to change the way the people in an organisation work together, but it can certainly be worth the trouble. The Courtesy System provides the framework for a better way of doing business.

The aim of the Courtesy System is to provide a framework for a 'Happiness-Centred Business': an environment where the business-family gain increased happiness and money by learning to receive pleasure from serving clients and fellow team members.

If we want our front line people to nurture and care for their customers, we must first create a warm, nurturing and caring atmosphere in the business family — a team member's politeness and warmth can appear false to a client unless warmth and politeness are normal in that organisation.

The team members will tend to treat their customers in the way that they are treated by their boss. It's like a family. When children who were abused by their parents reach adulthood themselves they often abuse the people that they control. I cringe when I hear powerful people telling their subordinates, in loud voice and no uncertain terms, that they must care for and be polite to the customers — or else!

132

If a team member's superiors in business use less courtesy towards the team member than the team member employs in his dealings with the client, then to the client observer the organisation appears incongruent. The politeness appears merely a veneer on the surface of an impolite and uncaring business.

 TREAT YOUR STAFF IN THE WAY THAT YOU WANT THEM TO TREAT YOUR CUSTOMERS.

I have found that the people who find it most hard to implement the Courtesy System are those in power. Those of us who live our business lives in authority over others often forget the common courtesies … and there is usually no one brave enough to draw our failings to our attention.

For this reason it is most important that the Courtesy System is implemented from the top down. It is unproductive to expect our business teams to take on any part of the system before we, the management, have learned to 'walk our talk'.

CHECK YOUR OWN BUSINESS

I have not found it very useful to ask the members of teams whether they are happy in their work. Almost everyone answers "Yes", even when they seem to be patently unhappy.

What people do is much more important than what they say, so it is interesting to walk around and observe what everyone is doing.

I have noticed that there are some indicators that tell me the happiness of people associated with your business. The indicators apply equally to team members, customers and suppliers.

- People stay a long time with your business — long-term team, customers and suppliers.
- People smile and laugh a lot.
- People do not complain constantly about their conditions, money, hours, standard of service, wages, bills etc.
- People come early and leave late. They like to spend time at your place of business.
- People talk with each other in a friendly way.
- People are polite to each other.
- People do not gossip and backbite.
- When you ask people about each other their comments are complimentary.

CHANGE CAN BE COMFORTABLE

Creating a business that gives great customer service necessitates a preoccupation with detail and a commitment to continued improvement.

The Courtesy System has helped us to feel comfortable with constant change in the service delivery systems that we utilise. The security of working in a warm and supportive environment leads to more comfort during times of change. Instead of everyone feeling threatened by something new, change becomes something to make our days more exciting — change becomes the desired norm.

We now enjoy change. We notice the benefits to ourselves and so we seek out changes.

Changes are no longer forced by management (me). Remember the old adage:

People like to change, they don't like to be changed!

Homage to New Ideas

It is very easy to think of a good reason why new ideas won't work.

We have adopted a strategy of dealing with new ideas. Now we feel that ideas are so delicate and fragile that, when they are first brought out into the light of day, they need protection. We do this by paying homage to new ideas and only saying positive things about them.

Before anyone is allowed to express any reservations, we insist on three positive reasons why the idea would work well and be beneficial to us. This system allows us to develop new ideas more quickly and easily than was the case when we always greeted new thought with, "Yes, but ...".

Please pay my ideas the compliment of thinking of good reasons why they should work in your organisation. Think of at least three reasons why each idea would be beneficial to your organisation before you discard it — please!

Management by Anger

The Courtesy System made it necessary to change some of my more dubious management methods.

135

I discovered that I used to use anger as a weapon. I didn't realise at the time that I was doing this, but nevertheless, it was part of my management tool bag.

I became angry when somebody did something I didn't approve of or didn't do what I wanted.

I still don't think I can control the first part of my anger, the part that makes me breathe faster, raises my blood pressure and dilates my pupils. It's just the adrenaline flowing in my veins. There were times, however, when I prolonged this effect and accentuated it, so that I could intimidate someone. I decided to 'do stress'.

I also remember, however, that I never displayed a lot of anger to someone whom I considered more powerful than myself — much too dangerous. Anger is something that most human beings and other animals will exhibit around subordinates, but not around superiors.

I always reserved my anger for those over whom I had some control. If a client annoyed me I would sometimes turn on a junior nurse whose only crime was to be powerless. I used anger as a weapon to punish and coerce. I don't do it any more.

For me, now that I live under the Courtesy System, it's no longer worth expressing anger. I know that because I have to follow the system, I will have to apologise afterwards. The apology costs me more pain than the pleasure I had from castigating someone.

I now realise that when I punish someone with my anger and they have to sublimate their anger, eventually they will either expend that anger on someone over whom they have power, or try to cause me some pain in a covert way.

If you ever use anger as a weapon you may like to learn the same lesson as I did. The momentary feeling of righteousness is not worth the damage to your stomach lining and heart muscle and it's not worth the damage you do to the organisation that you have helped to create.

If you can create an atmosphere where anger becomes unacceptable you will help yourself and everyone else around.

Management by Happiness

When my eldest daughter, Sarah, first came to work with Peter, the dentist who works with me, she had some difficulty getting used to the strangeness of the dental procedures.

Now, Sarah is great with people, but she had been doing the same job for a number of years and was not used to learning new manual skills. She found it stressful having to do so many things that were new to her. Sarah wasn't very happy and it was hard for Peter and the other care nurses with whom she had to work when she became stressed. She came to me with her problem and my initial suggestions were not very sympathetic and along the lines of 'Well it's just something you have to get used to. Work hard at it!'

I was uneasy with my 'business-like' solution and considered the whole question from the point of view of the happiness of those involved. I talked with Sarah again and we decided to allow her to do what we both thought would make her happiest — to take over more of Joanne's job of sterilising. Joanne then spent more time in the surgery, which made her happier; Sarah, free of the stress, more easily learned the surgery work that she had been finding so difficult. We had a bonus — everyone was happier.

Now when I look at a business problem the first thing I like to consider is the happiness of all concerned. I have learned that the decision that gives everyone the most happiness is usually the decision that is best for the business.

Team First!

It always struck me as strange that business people consider the customer as the most important element in their business.

For me, as strange and egotistical as it may seem, I am the most important person in my life ... and my business is part of my life. The people who are around me most — my Business-family — have more power to affect my happiness than the customers, so they (my Business-family) are the second most important people in my business. The customers come third.

Here is the idea behind 'Team First'.

 WHENEVER WE INTERACT WITH ANOTHER MEMBER OF THE TEAM, WE TREAT THEM AT LEAST AS WELL AS WE WOULD OUR BEST CUSTOMER.

The result of this is that everybody in the team feels worthwhile and important and part of the business family.

If there is ever a question of who to support — the customer or the team member — the support goes to the team person. In my business we have never had such a 'show down', but it is reassuring for the team to know what their position is, if it were to happen.

Children who grow up in a family where they are unconditionally loved and supported simply because they are part of the family, not because of how they perform, become strong, kind and assured adults.

Team members who know that they have the unconditional support of their peers and managers, are able to give more of themselves to their customers.

This does not mean that we feel that the team members are always right any more than the customer is always right. What it means is that we support those who are closest to us, whether we consider them right or wrong.

'Team First' has changed the way we work.

ANYONE FOR TEA?

One of the most obvious cultural changes that seemed to just happen is 'Anyone for tea?'

Whenever anyone decides that they are going to make a drink for themselves they ask everyone in the room if they also would like a drink — usually, "Anyone for tea?" because that's what we mostly drink.

We serve it to the customers in Royal Doulton china, on a silver tray with a silver teaspoon and strainer. At the last count we had 23 kinds of tea to offer.

When we make the tea for each other we serve it in the same way that we do to the clients and give the same choice of teas.

It seems like a little thing, to offer to serve one's colleagues, but it makes everyone feel very special and increases the bonds we feel with each other.

Team Comments

One of the best compliments I have had was from Michelle. We were chatting one day and she said: "You know, the best thing about working here is that it doesn't matter whether you are here or not, we still work in exactly the same way."

I don't know whether it meant the same thing to Michelle as to me, but I was definitely flattered. After all the work with systems to help everyone to be happy, to hear that it didn't matter whether I was around or not, meant that I had succeeded in empowering everyone. The motive force to provide awesome service now came from within the team members rather than from me.

Another comment came from a team member who had a pleasant house and home life: "It's nicer here than at home."

Team Driven Changes

It is impossible to write an operations manual that covers all situations. To give consistently 'awesome service', the business family needs to catch the right spirit, so that when there is no supervision and the task is not run-of-the-mill the customers still get wonderful service.

When the team members feel secure and happy among themselves they start to think of ways to make their customers happier. Indeed, they seem to start searching for the warm fuzzy feeling that comes from doing some new and innovative service that will delight their customers.

The Pill

Some time ago I asked Joanne if she would bring an analgesic pill for one of our clients.

We normally accompany such pills by a glass of ice water, with an ice cube that has been frozen around a small piece of fruit. It is then served in a long-stemmed glass, on a doily, on a Royal Doulton plate. This is all in the procedure manual — normal stuff. Joanne prepared the water and put the pill in its wrapping on the plate. She thought the pill did not look very elegant like that, bare on the plate, so she asked Kate what she thought could be done. Kate suggested she put the pill in one of the little flowered porcelain dishes in which we serve jam at the team breakfasts. Joanne presented it to the client. The dish with the pill sat elegantly on the plate, just as Kate had suggested. The customer said nothing, but she gave a little smile of pleasure to think someone had taken so much care for her. I am sure she thought, "If they take so much care presenting a pill, they surely must take incredible care when they do more important things in my mouth."

Joanne and Kate were happy because of the pleasure they had given. I was happy to see my team people empowered. The customer was happy to be elegantly served.

CLIENTS' COMMENTS

Client lying in the dental chair, talking about Kate, who had just kissed me goodbye and given Pat and Merilyn a goodbye hug: "I wish my kids were like that!"

Client in a lounge, drinking tea with me and listening to voices in other rooms: "People are always laughing here!"

HAPPINESS IS A TWO-WAY STREET

Not long ago at one of our Breakfasts we were talking together about our customers and how they have changed for the better and how good that makes us all feel.

We were thinking back to a period a few years ago and comparing the people we used to see with those we see now.

We all remembered that we had customers whose company we did not enjoy — people who were rude, frequently late, loud or impolite.

None of us could think of a present client who was like that.

Some of these people had left and some we had referred elsewhere, but many people seemed to have changed their character. They were now far more considerate in the way they treated us.

We discussed why this had happened and our thoughts went like this:

We have become a happier business-family.

We now understand how important happiness is to us and to others — our business aim now is to make our customers happier because of their association with us.

We have helped our clients to change the attitude with which they come to see us and there are now more happy customers around us. Because they are happier to be with us they treat us better.

People are coming early for their appointments so that they can spend time socialising with their Care Nurse. Everyone is smiling more and laughter has become common. This makes us, the team, feel wonderful.

We are giving happiness away to our customers and they are giving it back to us!

IT'S REALLY EASY ... WELL, NOT QUITE THAT EASY

So that's it — you just follow the Performance Standards and everything in your business will be wonderful. Well ... not quite. That would be too easy, and as one Australian Prime Minister once said, "Life isn't meant to be easy."

Business is certainly not that simple and there are many tasks quite unrelated to courtesy that must be performed before a business runs prosperously and happily. My team and I have spent a lot of time and effort developing other systems to increase efficiency and improve profits, but none have approached the Courtesy System in fulfilling our basic need for happiness.

To implement the Courtesy System takes time and no small effort. However, for us, in our little corner of the universe it has been well worth the energy we have expended. The Courtesy System has been the core of our transition from being unhappy in our business to actually receiving happiness from our business.

Thank you for staying with me to the end. I hope you try building a Happiness-Centred Business for yourself. Work at it, and your own corner of the universe will become a more pleasant place to spend your life.

Paddi Lund

EPILOGUE

ince *Building the Happiness-Centred Business* was first published in 1994 — without a lot of fanfare — Paddi's story has found its way onto the bookshelves of many business people through-out the world, even though it is not available in any bookshops.

Paddi insisted on a 'referral-only' distribution, and here at Solutions Press, we were a little concerned. We believed that many people could benefit from Paddi's unique philosophies, but how would they manage to obtain their copy of the book? How would we recoup our investment? Our fears have proved groundless. Indeed, as you see, it has been necessary to print this second edition of the book. I would not be at all surprised if there were a third.

We are very grateful to those readers who have recommended Paddi's *Building the Happiness-Centred Business* and made this method of distribution possible. We are constantly surprised by the warmth of the comments we hear from those who have been recommended to the book — usually about the delightful way in which Paddi's unusual ideas and lucid style have been described.

A Most Unusual Business

Paddi has built an 'invitation only' business — a business which thrives in spite of a locked front door, no signage and an ex-directory telephone number. And he has created a system that educates his customers to the benefits of his products and services so well that that they do his advertising for him, and ensure he has a constant flow of desirable new customers.

Paddi has developed such unusual and effective financial systems that he has virtually no bad debts and a negative accounts receivable — his customers are happy to pay for their services as they are rendered ... and often weeks in advance!

We often hear from those who make the pilgrimage to see Paddi's offices for themselves that the atmosphere in the building is so warm that they feel at home as soon as they are greeted at the door ... and this is a Dental business!

There is a large cappuccino machine, a multitude of types of teas and coffees, an oven to bake 'dental buns' that creates the familiar aroma of fresh baking ... and nary a sign of a front desk. All of this has been carefully designed and systematised to achieve just the result that Paddi desires — a consistent supply of friendly happy customers.

Is it Possible?

You may well ask, could a business like Paddi describes actually exist? Could it possibly be true what Paddi has said about his business? Who better to answer this question than those who have visited his office and seen for themselves.

Paul Dunn tells it this way:

> He's totally redefined what it means to be 'in business'. Paddi's built what to my mind is one of the most astonishing businesses on the planet.

Mike Basch visited twice:

> Paddi's understanding of his own nature and what that tells him about the rest of us has enabled him to build an amazing business. In fact, the most outrageous, by many standards the most successful, and certainly the happiest dental practice in the world.

145

> *Paddi has showed me that it's the simple things that truly make the difference in business. A cup of tea brewed with care. A simple 'please' and 'thank you' said from the heart. And that 'less is more'. The fewer hours you work, the more money you make. The less you try to sell the more customers want to buy. When you lock your doors, more people want to come in.*
>
> *It all sounds a little crazy, but I can tell you, it works. Take Paddi's principles on-board and you can certainly make more money, work less time and have more fun.*

Brad Sugars also visited Paddi:

> *Paddi has truly created something amazing. Business can be one of three things in your life, an absolute headache that you run yourself, something you get other people to run for you, or as Paddi so eloquently shows, it can be an amazingly wonderful part of your life.*

Brian Sher as well:

> *Paddi was overworked, underpaid and depressed. His business life a stressful, daily grind. Now he runs one of Australia's happiest most successful dental practices, with an incredible culture of customer service. Paddi is one of the most relaxed and stress-free business people I know — an inspiration to thousands of others.*

We have persuaded Paddi to write about some of his systems for business, and you may expect to see some of these publications in the near future. In the meantime if you have the opportunity to hear Paddi in one of the rare times he speaks, take it. You will be glad you did.

Paddi in Public

As I mentioned earlier in this text, Paddi does not like to leave his comfortable happy business, so it is hard to persuade him to travel and present his ideas in public. So how do people receive his message at his infrequent presentations? Rich Madow hosted a 'Super-Seminar' in Las Vegas at which Paddi was a speaker:

> What a pleasure it was. Paddi is just as genuine, warm and humble in person as he is in print, and his message was as well received as any I have ever heard. When Paddi spoke, calmly and quietly, to a room of almost one thousand people, you could have heard a pin drop. Even the cameramen and stage technicians were following in awe. His concepts were so simple, so obvious, yet until that moment they just seemed foreign and almost inanely ridiculous. What an eye-opener!

Helen Parker invited Paddi to the UK to speak for a day:

> I had the very real pleasure of meeting Paddi and introducing him to many of my clients. To me this was one of life's great treats. Paddi showed us (and he illustrates this beautifully with his stories) that if you are not enjoying your life, change it. You really can.

Paul Dunn also was impressed with Paddi's appearance at his marketing 'Boot Camps':

> I've had the privilege of working with Paddi before literally thousands of people now. Every single one of them has gained insights they never thought they would.

In Conculusion

A few final words from the business authorities:

Helen Parker: Paddi is a gentle, modest, unassuming man who gives you the heart to believe that if he can do it, anyone can. He is an inspiration to everyone, whatever walk of life

Brian Sher: If you want to achieve a work-life like Paddi's, just study and apply the ideas in this sensational book.

Chris Newton: Paddi was prepared to take risks in baring his soul to help others to 'save' theirs. That takes guts. I think the gamble has paid off.

147

Omer Reed: *'Building the Happiness-Centred Business' is an extraordinary story. Paddi has committed himself to the happiness game. Join him!*

Mike Basch: *If there is such a thing as an ideal way to live that combines happiness and success, I believe Paddi has discovered it. Apply Paddi's simple philosophies and you will create a unique business where customers love to buy, employees love to work and owners make lots of money. Would you want more?*

Paul Dunn: *The journey is, as Paddi says, one of creating happiness for ourselves. This book does that. Read it. Use it. It might just add more life to your life as well.*

Jay Abraham: *I admire what Paddi Lund has done with his life. I admire what he is trying to do to help others.*

Rich Madow: *This book changed my life forever. It is one of the most wonderful books I have ever read. Paddi, thank you, thank you, thank you!*

We are happy to have been able to publish *Building the Happiness-Centred Business*. We hope you have enjoyed (and benefited) from it, and we would like to give you our best wishes for your happiness in business

Fletcher Potanin, Editor
On behalf of all at Solutions Press

HAPPINESS & PROFIT

THE PADDI SERIES

The Absolutely
Critical
Non-Essentials

BY DR PADDI LUND

Business Happiness and Money

Paddi worked hard to build his small service business, but found he was miserable. His solution: Paddi made 'happiness' the focus of his business and made systems so that critical areas of customer contact worked automatically. Paddi achieved his goal of happiness in business and earned greater profits in the process!

Extra-ordinary Innovation

Paddi is writing the detailed story of his six most important business systems. Now you can read all about Paddi's extra-ordinary innovation in the areas of customer service, marketing and organisational harmony. You'll discover the power of these six simple business systems, and why they are essential to your success.

Read the rest of the *Paddi Series*

Now as 'Works-in-Progress' Special Reports, each US$79 (UK£59, A$99)

The Absolutely Critical Non-Essentials

Simple systems for the 'Little Things' that will impress customers with your quality and will help create an experience about which customers will rave.

Mobilising Your Customer Sales Force

How Paddi made an incredible referral system and thrived! 'A' Class customers on-tap with no advertising!

Simply Stunning Customer Service

Build profitable, long-term customer relationships with a smaller team, less effort and amazing customer care.

The Secret of Customers Who Love to Pay

Customers who pay on time and enjoy it? Paddi helps you to build trust (and profits) with the 'Buying Cycle'.

Training Customers to Treasure Your Business

How Paddi uses a simple system of education so that customers value his services, are anxious to buy ... and happily pay what he asks.

Business Happiness Package #1

We have collected each of the *Special Reports* in a package for extra value. You'll also receive as our gift a copy of *Building the Happiness-Centred Business* a *Courtesy System Plaque* plus an audio tape set of Paddi telling his story live. A value of US$514 for **Total US$395**

Use the order form overleaf or visit **www.solutionspress.com.au**

Solutions Press 149 Old Cleveland Road Capalaba, Qld 4157 Australia

Telephone (+61-7) 3823 3230
Facsimile (+61-7) 3390 3610

☑ **Yes!** I want to read about Paddi's other Business Systems. Please send me these *Special Reports– Works-in-Progress* for US$79, UK£59 or A$99 each (plus shipping)...

- ❏ *Mobilising Your Customer Sales Force*
- ❏ *The Absolutely Critical Non-Essentials*
- ❏ *Simply Stunning Customer Service*
- ❏ *The Secret of Customers Who Love to Pay*
- ❏ *Training Customers to Treasure Your Business*

❏ **Yes!** I want a business where we work efficiently, make more money and enjoy ourselves. *Business Happiness Package #1* will show me the way. (Shipping is US$60, A$29, UK£35) Send me...

Mobilising Your Customer Sales Force   *Simply Stunning Customer Service*
The Absolutely Critical Non-Essentials   *Customers Who Love to Pay*
Training Customers to Treasure Your Business

Plus, with our compliments for your team...
1 of *Building the Happiness Centred Business* (Value US$20)
1 *Courtesy System Action Plaque* (Value US$20)
The Original Paddi Story audio tape set (Value US$79)
(A value of US$514 for...) **Total US$395 (UK£295 A$495)**

Name: _____

Business: _____

Address: _____

_____ FOL _____

Telephone: MAR 1 5 2024 _____ Fax: _____

E-mail: _____ Web: _____

I would like to pay with: ❏ The cheque I've included,
❏ My Credit Card. Type: _____ Expiry: _____

Card Number: _____

Name on Card: _____

Website: www.solutionspress.com.au   E-mail: loretta@solutionspress.com.au